legacy of the cat

THE ULTIMATE ILLUSTRATED GUIDE

revised and expanded

BY **GLORIA STEPHENS**

PHOTOGRAPHS BY **TETSU YAMAZAKI**

CHRONICLE BOOKS
SAN FRANCISCO

Contents

First published in Japan by Yama-Kei Publishers Co., Ltd.
Library of Congress Cataloging in Publication Data available upon request.
ISBN 0-8118-2910-3

Printed in Japan
Cover design: Sara Schneider

Distributed in Canada by
Raincoast Books
9050 Shaughnessy Street
Vancouver, British Columbia V6P 6E5
10 9 8 7 6 5 4 3 2 1

Chronicle Books LLC
85 Second Street
San Francisco, CA 94105

www.chroniclebooks.com

Profiles of Cats: 51 Breeds

Introduction

In September 1997, Tetsu informed me we would make a second *Legacy of the Cat.* Wonderful, I thought; it should be easy to do the text. I was very wrong. I had one year to complete the text. I sat and stared at a blank computer monitor for months. What was I going to say? This was worse than starting a painting. I have, in the past, stared at a blank canvas for a long time before putting the first mark on it. This was just about the same.

After approaching the new text from different angles, I decided to go more into the history of the breeds. This should be documented anyway.

Tetsu came to my home in Oregon in September of 1998 to visit and get started working together on *Legacy of the Cat II.* I showed Tetsu the graphics from the molecular genetics book I was also working on. He liked them and asked if I would include some of the graphics in this book. I agreed, only with the understanding that I could use them in my other book that has not been published yet. He assured me there would be no problem. The line drawings of the breeds of cats, charts, and graphics for the Genetics portion of this book are from my molecular genetics book that I have been working on off and on for the past seven years. They were done in Corel Draw, starting with a line or a circle.

May I please add a disclaimer here? I am not a professional research geneticist. My basic knowledge of genetics I learned in college, but there are no degrees in Domestic Feline Genetics.

I was privileged to first learn domestic feline genetics from

the great Don Shaw. Don was an Allbreed Judge for ACFA and then TICA. He was a geneticist of great knowledge that he freely shared with all of us. Don was my friend, my teacher, and my advocate. He died on Christmas day several years ago; I miss him. The rest of my knowledge has come from breeders, studying pedigrees, and doing some of the breedings myself.

I would like to dedicate this book to Don Shaw's memory.

This book, as was the first *Legacy,* is based on TICA Rules, as it would have been impossible for me to know the Standards or Rules of the other organizations. I will offer you new theories concerning the White Spotting Gene and the Inhibitor Gene. They work on paper; they work on "This is what we see, now how do we get it."

I have included a very small offering of molecular genetics in this book. Why? Maybe, just maybe with a basic understanding, you will marvel, as I do, when a kitten is born alive and healthy.

Tetsu is an absolute marvel to watch at work. He is so patient with the cats. He can do things with them that I am not sure many other photographers can do. He catches them in motion. He makes the cats come to life in the photographs.

This time, the book has gone much faster than the first *Legacy* as before I was limited to an old CPM80 (it was not a graphics computer). Also, when I first moved to Oregon, I lived 6500 feet on top of a mountain with no electricity and a generator. I lived there for one year. I now live on the side of a mountain, but only up about 2500 feet with electricity. I now have six computers (Windows OS, MAC, and Linux); all of the latest software; and the Internet. I own my own domain name. When Yama Kei Publishing Company needed something from me, they e-mailed me. I was either able to e-mail the answer right back to them, or put a graphic or text on a Web page for them to take. With the first *Legacy,* everything had to be done by regular mail or visits to Japan. We speeded up all of this with the use of e-mail and the Internet.

Tetsu has sent me (on CDs) over 2000 photos. I had to view each one and choose the photos to be used in this book. Last time, I had to go to Tokyo to view his photos.

So, instead of having to make the six trips to Japan, as I did with the first *Legacy of the Cat,* I have not had to make a single trip.

When Tetsu told me the translation into Japanese had begun, I was excited. When Chronicle Books (the San Francisco publishing company) sent me this manuscript to edit, it was exciting and frightening at the same time, in knowing—this is it. *Legacy of the Cat II* is a reality; my text will be put into print and will be read by thousands of people throughout the world. I consider this to be an awesome and humbling experience.

Tetsu and I wanted to leave you with a legacy of the domestic feline in the first book. We want to continue to leave you with a legacy of knowledge and beauty of the cat. These books have been a true labor of love for both of us.

Dear Readers, I sincerely hope you enjoy this new book as much as Tetsu and I have enjoyed preparing it for you.

Gloria Stephens

Evolution of Cats

The Cat in Ancient Times

More than fifty million years ago, a small, weasel-like animal called the *Miacis* roamed the earth. Most scientists now believe that this animal was the ancestor of today's domestic cat, as well as the raccoon, dog, and bear. It was about forty million years ago that members of the cat family first appeared.

It is believed that the cat was first domesticated some 5,000 years ago in the valley of the Nile, in Upper Egypt. These small domesticated African wildcats were valued for their skill in hunting pests such as snakes, rats, and mice. The people in this valley were farmers and depended on grain as the mainstay of their diet. Vermin were attracted to the grain, and the cats were attracted to the vermin. The Egyptians undoubtedly offered the cats a steady supply of food in addition to the vermin and made every effort to encourage the cats to continue to protect the grain and not return to the wild. Cats know a good thing when they find it—plenty of food, nice vermin, and a safe environment free of predatory wild animals—so they moved in and stayed.

As Egyptian society developed, the numbers of people in urban centers grew, and grain production increased. Domestic cats, many of which were used to protect the grain in storage facilities, were now being kept as beloved household pets. But the cities were growing and there were lots of storage buildings filled with grain. The rodents multiplied to the point that one of the early Pharaohs realized he needed more cats in order to control the rodent populations. He knew, however, that the people would not be happy to give up their adored pets. So the story goes, the Pharaoh, who himself was revered as a now living god, decided to make the cats demigods. Since it would be unthinkable for a mere human to own a demigod, the Pharaoh would be the owner of these small deities. The humans most certainly could provide shelter and food for the new demigods and, as part of their ritual worship, each caretaker would be required to bring his cats to an assigned granary each night and pick them up each morning. Thus, the cats were looked upon as dependents, and the caretakers were given a benefit in the form of a tax break.

The cat was so valuable in ancient Egyptian society that laws were enacted making it a capital crime to kill or injure a cat. If there was a fire in a home, the cats were saved first, then the humans. If a cat died, the human household went into deep mourning. The family members would cry, shave their eyebrows, and beat their breasts to display their grief. So greatly loved were the cats that when they died,

they were mummified and placed in special cemeteries. In the twentieth century such a cemetery, containing more than three hundred thousand mummified cats, was found in an excavation at Beni Hassan.

The Egyptians carried their reverence for the cat even further. The goddess of life and family, Bastet, was depicted with the body of a woman and the head of a cat. In her left hand, she held an amulet with the "all-seeing eye," or *utchat*. Because of the cat's connection with the goddess Bastet, the household cat was believed to have the power to protect its family from disease and injuries.

In ancient Egypt the word for cat was *mau* (which sounds like "meow"). However, the word *utchat* seems to be the origin of the vast majority of names for the cat: *cat, chat, cattus, gatus, gatous, gato, katt, katte, kitte,* and *kitty*. The name of the cat-goddess Bastet became Pasht in later Egyptian times (during the reign of the Ptolemaic kings); from the name Pasht derived many other names for the cat: *pasht, past, pushd, pusst, puss,* and *pussy*.

Since it was a capital crime to take a cat from the Pharaoh, the domesticated cat remained in Egypt for a very long time. However, when the Egyptian ships sailed up and down the Nile River, cats were brought along on these ships in order to protect the precious grain on board. When ships reached the mouth of the Nile and unloaded their grain, cats found their way off the vessels and onto others, eventually being taken to various countries on the Mediterranean Sea. Domestic cats also were taken by traders to India, Burma, Siam, and China around 1500 BC. It was not, however, until the Persian, Greek, and Roman conquests of Egypt that the cat lost its deified status, thus allowing the cat to spread throughout the empires of Darius, Alexander, and Caesar.

Cats first came to Europe and the Middle East about 1000 B.C., most likely on the ships of Greek and Phoenician traders. Like the Egyptians, the ancient Greeks and Romans also valued cats for their ability to control vermin. In Rome (around 900 B.C.), the cat was considered the guardian spirit of a household and was the symbol of liberty and freedom. Romans called the cat *felis,* meaning "good omen."

In their travels throughout their empire, the Romans brought cats to Britain. Since cats were needed onboard ships in order to control rodents, they went wherever the ships went, becoming established all over Europe, including Norway.

The Cat During the Middle Ages

In the Middle Ages, the Norse goddess Freya was depicted as riding in a chariot pulled by two large cats. The Christians were soon to bar the worship of her and her cats; they considered Freya to be a demon, and her cats were therefore thought to be a manifestation of the devil.

As Christianity took hold across Europe during the Middle Ages, the cat became the object of superstition. During this period, hundreds of thousands of cats throughout Europe were tortured and killed, and many thousands of people were executed merely for keeping or protecting cats. As a result, the cat population reportedly was reduced to almost nothing.

Naturally, killing off the cats meant the return of the vermin. This time, not only did the vermin eat the grain, they also carried with them the plague or "Black Death." Almost one-fourth of the entire human population in Europe, in the 1300s, was wiped out by the plague.

While the epidemic raged, the killing of cats was temporarily abandoned, and cats were given a chance to replenish their numbers. The increased cat population began to consume the plague-carrying rats, thus helping to reduce the numbers of infected vermin, and the Black Death began to loosen its grip. Once the plague subsided in Europe, the persecution of cats resumed; cats were now identified as witches. In 1484, Pope Innocent VIII denounced the cat and all who housed it.

Despite the superstitions surrounding cats, they remained a necessity for keeping vermin under control, especially on ships. As a result, the cat began a widespread migration to the seaports of the world. Domestic cats spread throughout Asia, where in some countries they would become valued for their ability to protect silkworm cocoons from rodents. The people of the Orient greatly admired the mystery and beauty of the cat, and many writers and artists in Japan and China depicted these animals in their art. In Burma and Siam it was believed that the souls of departed people lived in the bodies of sacred cats before moving on to the next life. Cats lived in the temples and palaces of Siam (now Thailand). And in Japan religious ceremonies for the souls of departed cats were sometimes held.

During the 1600s and the 1700s, traders, explorers, colonists, and settlers brought cats with them as they traveled to the New World. Many of the cats in North America today are descendants of these cats.

The Cat in Modern Times

The first cat show was held in London in 1871. The first cat association, the

National Cat Club of Great Britain, was formed in 1887. Like today's cat associations, it registered purebred cats by recording the ancestries (pedigrees) of the animals to ensure the preservation of the breeds. These associations also sponsor cat shows and establish the standards for judging of each breed. Breeders and pet owners display their finest cats at these shows, where the cats compete in groups based on factors such as breed, age, and sometimes sex. Highly trained judges at these shows award points for how well each cat meets the standards of its breed, and cats earning the highest numbers of points may become champions.

Cats have lived with kings and presidents. Abraham Lincoln, Theodore Roosevelt, Calvin Coolidge, Herbert Hoover, Ronald Reagan, and Bill Clinton all have owned cats. Both Napoleon's conqueror, the Duke of Wellington, and Queen Victoria kept cats, and France's Cardinal Richelieu provided for the care of his fourteen cats in his will. Certain Japanese and Chinese emperors, and Louis XV of France, favored white cats.

Superstitions about cats persist even today, such as the legend of the cat's nine lives. Another legend from Europe's Middle Ages has it that on every black cat there is a single white hair; in France it is said that this white hair will bring wealth or love to the per-

son who can remove it without the cat scratching him. A common superstition in North America is that a black cat crossing one's path brings bad luck, but in Great Britain black cats are thought to bring good luck.

Today the elegant, graceful cat is a popular house pet throughout the world. One of the most intelligent of the domesticated animals, the cat is independent and difficult to train. Cats are valued for their gentle, affectionate natures, but their loyalty must be earned; cats won't stay where they are mistreated. They respond to loving owners with loyalty, affection, and respect.

Cats are noted for their keen sense of smell, their sharp hearing, and their ability to see in near darkness. Their large, striking eyes, fastidious cleanliness, and exotic looks are greatly admired. Perhaps Leonardo da Vinci best described the cat, calling it "Nature's masterpiece."

The Lure of Wild Cats

Of all God's creatures there is only one that cannot be made the slave of the leash. That creature is the cat. All cats, wild or domestic, have a similar skeleton with compact, round skull; long backbone; and (usually) a long tail. The body proportions and bone structure of the wildcat vary from breed to breed, reflecting their adaptations to different environments. There are several things to take into consideration before acquiring a wildcat for a pet.

• Check with your state wildlife board and find out their requirements for your state.

• Acquire one from an experienced breeder who has taken the time to hand raise the cub from the time that it is about 10 days old.

• Check into the personalities and the needs of the breed in which you are interested.

• Remember that all little animals are cute, but as adults they may grow up to be big and powerful wildcats. There are a few that can live in a home with people, but many cannot.

• Wildcats should be altered at an early age, before the sex hormones kick in.

• Most breeders of wildcats suggest that the cats be declawed at an early age.

• Many wildcats require special diets, in most cases, raw meat.

• Make certain you have a vet who can (and will) treat a wildcat.

Serval

In my opinion, the Serval is one of the most beautiful of the wildcats. Everything is extreme about this cat. It has a long body, long legs, and a spotted pattern. Mature Servals are from 24 to 36 inches long, with their tails measuring from $1/3$ to $1/2$ of the head length. They may weigh between 20 and 40 pounds. The ground color varies from a tan to an orange, with dark brown to black spots that are uniquely in rows on the sides of the torso and stripes on the back. The tail may have several rings of color and ends in a black tail tip. One of the outstanding features is their large funnel-shaped ears that are rimmed with black and have a large white spot on the back of each ear. The Serval is perhaps one of the most graceful of all the cats; it is agile and can make high jumps with no effort.

Servals may be kept as pets only if they have been hand raised as cubs. These are to be considered high-energy cats and their owners need to know where they are at all times, as they can also get into things that might harm the cat. Therefore, the household must be made cat proof—any toxic chemicals must be removed, including pesticides that could poison the cat. If they have not been declawed, the claws can destroy your furniture or, worse yet, hurt a human while the cat is "at play."

Because these are high-energy cats, they must have plenty of exercise. It goes without saying that these cats must never be left alone with strangers, especially children.

African Serval

Lynx

Lynx

The Canadian Lynx weighs between 15 and 35 pounds. The males are, of course, larger than the females. They have a long body, and large pointed ears that end in very thick tufts of hair. The ground color may be a light brownish gray to a yellow gray, while the tips of the hairs may appear to be silvered. They may or may not have dark spots of color scattered throughout their coat. The coat is very thick and dense; there is a "ruff" of hair just under the neck. The tail is short—2 to 5 inches in length. They have a broad, puffy muzzle and a broad nose. This is a long-legged cat with feet that are almost oversized for the legs.

Most Lynx are not suitable as house cats, especially if they have not been altered or hand raised with care. If they have not been altered, they will spray or mark your house and furniture. They have also been known to be temperamental. As with any wildcat in captivity, it is essential that the owner try to understand the breed, and to understand that a wildcat that has not been properly hand raised and trained by the breeder will never make a good pet.

Bobcat

The Bobcat is found on the North American continent. It ranges from central Mexico to southern Canada, living in a variety of environments. It has the ability to adapt to many living conditions; it does not, however, like wet or desert environments. It prefers heavy brush, as well as wooded or forest areas.

The Bobcat is not a large cat, being of 2 to 3 1/2 feet in length. The tail is short and stubby, measuring from 4 to 7 inches in length. The tail ends in a black tip of color. Bobcats may weigh from 10 to 30 pounds.

The eyes are rather unique in that they are rather small for the head and are set back under a heavy brow line, giving a "straight across" look to the top of the eye—a wild look indeed! The muzzle is wide and puffy; the nose is broad.

The coat color ranges from buff to a light brown and is marked with dark brown or black spots of various sizes. The ears are marked with black on the back and may or may not end in a black tuft. They do have what we in the cat fancy call "mutton chops"— the hair that extends from the ears to the corner of the mouth.

Bobcat

This cat is a good climber, although it prefers to spend much of its time on the ground.

As with any wildcat, Bobcats may not make good pets when they are adults.

Asian Leopard Cat

The Asian Leopard Cat is not much larger than the domestic cat, but the legs are longer. The head is relatively small for the length of the body. The muzzle is short and narrow. The eyes are huge, as it is a nocturnal cat. The body length varies from 25 to 32 inches, with a thick tail that varies in

Asian Leopard Cat

length from 11 to 14 inches. The males will weigh more than the females, with weights that vary from 7 to 15 pounds.

The breed is known for the lovely markings that may be spotted, rosetted, or sometimes marbled. The tail either has rings of color or is spotted. The tip of the tail is black. The underside of the cat is whitish.

These are solitary, nocturnal cats that do not make good pets. They do not like to be touched by humans, and are meat eaters, so it isn't safe to leave them with other pets.

Genetics

What makes a black cat blue? What makes a blue Persian different from a brown tabby Maine Coon different from a white Cornish Rex? What makes a cat different from a dog? It is all in the genes.

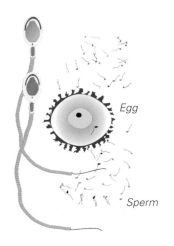

Egg

Sperm

Cells, Genes, and Chromosomes

Our bodies are made up of cells, each containing a nucleus, or command center. The nucleus controls the functions of the cell itself (whether it be a nerve cell, heart cell, skin cell, sperm cell, or egg cell). Chromosomes are contained within the nucleus, and on the chromosomes are genes, arranged like bands on a string. A gene actually

Crossing Over

consists of nucleotides that are held together on the DNA molecule. These nucleotides consist of only four amino acids: adenine, cytosine, guanine, and thymine. A and C attract each other; G and T attract each other. It is how these nucleotides are lined up on the chromosome that will "spell" out the recipe to make a protein. These same

amino acids are present in all living creatures. Just these four nucleotides do everything and make a black cat blue. What makes us different from the cat? Again, it is the way the nucleotides are lined up, the order of the nucleotides on the chromosome, that make the difference. There may be millions of nucleotides on a chromosome.

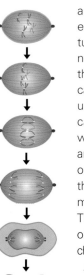

Mitosis

A chromosome is one single molecule of DNA (deoxyribonucleic acid). Each cell in the domestic cat has 38 chromosomes, or 19 pairs. The chromosomes are in the form of a double helix. The actual instructions for the domestic cat may be considered to consist of two sets of 19 books each. An offspring will receive 19 chromosomes from each parent, so that when the egg is fertilized, the full complement of 38, or 19 pairs of, chromosomes is restored. There are two special chromosomes which are called the sex chromosomes. In our domestic cat, phaeomelanin (red) is located on the

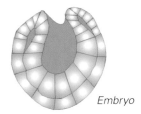

Embryo

X chromosome. It should be noted that the Y chromosome does not carry color. Each chromosome consists of light- and dark-colored bands, or genes. Genes control a single feature or a group of features in the makeup of an individual; yet it must also be understood that many of the genes interact with other genes, and that there are sub-genes (polygenes) that influence the major genes. There are far more possible instructions from the DNA in

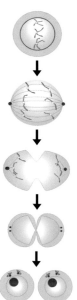

Meiosis

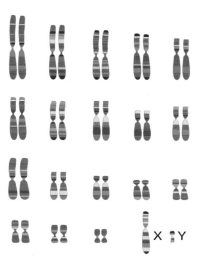

X Y

38 Chromosomes of the Domestic Feline

12

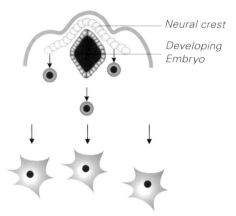

Melanoblasts develop into Melanocytes

one single chromosome than there are atoms in the known universe.

Like a set of blueprints, the genome, or the sum total of all the genes in an individual, contains all the information needed to build the individual, and the specific combination of genes determines what characteristics will be passed from generation to generation.

There are two copies of each gene, one for each paired chromosome (S/S; S/s; or s/s). These paired genes are called alleles.

Two Types of Cell Division

Meiosis or Germ Cell Division
This is when the egg and the sperm have a haploid half the required number of chromosomes. This must be, because when the sperm fertilizes the egg, the full complement of chromosomes are restored. Genetic information (from both parents) is passed down from generation to generation in this type of cell division.

Mitosis Cell Division
The other type of cell division is body or autosomal (mitosis), in which the body cells divide so that each daughter cell will have the exact same number of chromosomes and the same chromosomes as did the parent cell.

In the domestic feline, haploid = 19 chromosomes as in the germ cells (sperm and the egg); the body (autosomal) cells have 38 chromosomes.

Crossing Over
During the early meiotic germ cell division, there is an interchange of part of one chromosome with the corresponding part for the other chromosome. Parts of like chromosomes sort of play musical chairs; they cross over, they exchange genes. This crossing over is extremely important, as it adds variety to the genes an individual may inherit and it also explains why no two individuals are exactly alike (unless they are twins from the same fertilized egg).

X and the Y Chromosomes
It is also important to understand that females have two X chromosomes. It is the double X that makes them females. The male has one X chromosome and one Y chromosome–this is one unmatched pair. It is the male that determines the sex of the offspring. When the chromosomes line up in pairs during meiosis, the Y chromosome does not have a "like" chromosome to line up with; the X chromosome will have another X to pair up with. The Y chromosome determines the sex only; it does not have

information as to color, pattern, etc. If either cat is a red or the female is a tortie, then we are dealing with the sex-linked red gene and the male will get its color from its mother's X chromosome.

Embryo
The fertilized egg starts out as only one cell. This cell divides into two, the two divide into four, and so on until there is the "shell" of a living creature. The cells of the embryo began to differentiate and divide in such a way as to form a "hollow" ball at first. The hollow ball of cells then flattens in on itself, forming two rows of cells. The folded two rows of cells fold again. This process is repeated, until the once hollow ball is filled with cells. The beginnings of life form. The top cells are the Epidermal Ectoderm. The Neural Crest is formed under these cells.

Melanoblast Migration
The melanoblasts migrate from the neural crest during early embryonic development. The melanoblasts become

13

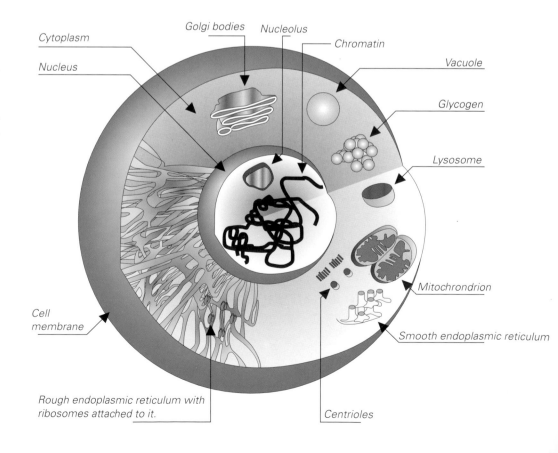

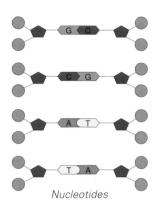
Nucleotides

melanocytes. The melanocytes that are responsible for ear, eye, skin, and hair pigmentation are called melanosomes and are pigment factories. In the melanocytes there is an enzyme named tyrosinase. This enzyme has only one job in its life: to oversee and make melanin. This migration is under genetic control.

Dominant and Recessive Genes

Genes are either dominant, co-dominant, or recessive. Co-dominant means the effects of both alleles at a particular locus are apparent. In the homozygous state (B/B or b/b), the two allelic genes are alike; the same message is sent–in this instance, B/B to make black pigment or b/b to make chocolate pigment. In the heterozygous state (B/b), the two allelic genes are different from each other. The dominant gene is in control; the recessive (b) is carried and may have little or no effect over the dominant gene (B). In this instance the message would be

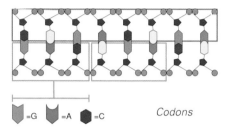

=G   =A   =C

Codons

The nucleotides are read in groups of threes. Each codon codes for an amino acid. If the "reading" starts at the wrong place, it will code for the wrong amino acid. This is called a silent mutation. There are other types of mutations given in this chapter.

B/b–to make black pigment. In the presence of a dominant gene, the recessive gene of the same allele is a null gene, or not operative. It is dominated or overshadowed by a stronger gene and not allowed to express itself. In order for a recessive gene to express itself, each parent must have the recessive gene to give to its offspring.

Recessive genes can remain hidden for generations. The presence of recessive genes can explain why unexpected colors, hair lengths and textures, or other physical attributes appear in a litter of kittens.

A domestic cat is either red, as a result of phaeomelanin (red-yellow) pigment granules in the hair shaft, or it is not red, as a result of eumelanin (black-brown) granules in the hair shaft. Phaeomelanin is not dominant over eumelanin. Phaeomelanin is sex-linked; it is positioned on the "X" chromosome. I use the symbol X^P for phaeomelanin and X for Eumelanin, as it is not sex-linked.

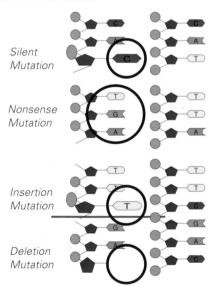

Silent Mutation

Nonsense Mutation

Insertion Mutation

Deletion Mutation

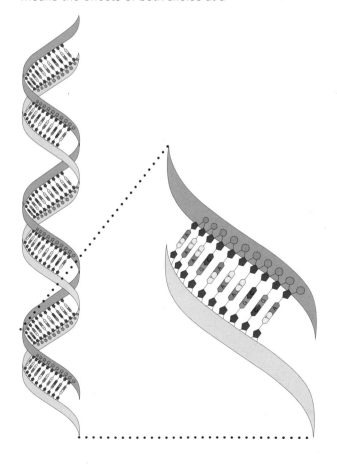

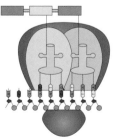

Ribosome

tRNA (the yellow images above) pick up the correct amino acids and take them to the Ribosomes (the brown image). Met, Asp, and Ile are examples of amino acids. They are abbreviations of Methionine, Aspartic Acid, and Isoleucine, respectively.

Double Helix

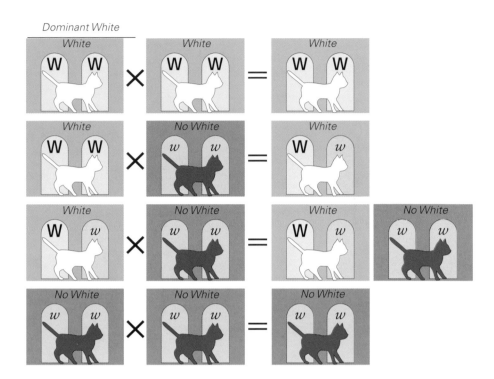

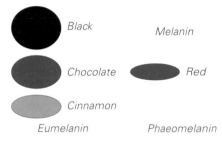

Black — Chocolate — Cinnamon

Eumelanin

Melanin — Red

Phaeomelanin

The gene for a eumelanin color is part of the genotype of a red or cream-colored cat, but to the best of my knowledge, has no effect on the red coloration. Black-red, chocolate-red, or cinnamon-red should not be possible. Black granules are football in shape; chocolate granules are football shaped but not as plump as the black granules; cinnamon granules are less plump than the chocolate granules.

Phaeomelanin granules are spiracle in shape.

If a cat has banded or ticked hairs (see diagram), it has the dominant agouti gene (A). This gene is responsible for the alternating dark and light agouti bands on the hairs. The non-agouti gene (a/a) is responsible for the solid colors, or "self" colors.

The result of the agouti gene is an on-off system of protein synthesis which is created by the action of a protein molecule called the agouti peptide and a hormone called the Melanocyte Stimulating Hormone (MSH).

The agouti peptide has its own receptor on the melanocyte. When the peptide is on its receptor, shredded or weakened phaeomelanin is made; eumelanin production is halted. When the agouti peptide leaves its receptor, MSH is able to stimulate the melanocyte into producing eumelanin; phaeomelanin production is halted.

Melanocytes are pigment cells that transfer their products, the melanosomes, to the hair bulbs; melanosomes are responsible for the number, size, type, and distribution of pigment particles. Within the melanocytes, melanin is formed after the enzyme tyrosinase reactions occur in the melanosomes.

Therefore, alternating bands of eumelanin and phaeomelanin are produced as the result of the melanocyte being alternately stimulated by either the agouti peptide or the Melanocyte Stimulating Hormone.

Phaeomelanin synthesis is complex and involves several genes. Agouti, however, is made locally in the hair follicle.

If a cat is of a solid color, it has the recessive non-agouti genes (a/a). These genes work only with eumelanin; a solid-colored cat is eumelanin only. Therefore, phaeomelanin is inoperative when the non-agouti gene is present.

Eumelanin solid-colored kittens and young adult cats, especially blacks, blues, and chocolates, may go through several color changes before their ultimate coat color comes in, and may display tabby markings called "ghost tabby markings" that will usually vanish when adulthood is reached.

All red or cream-colored cats will show a tabby pattern to some extent. The reason for this is that in a phaeomelanin (red) cat, no eumelanin is present. Since the non-agouti gene works only on eumelanin, banding and tabby pattern will show up on a phaeomelanin (red) cat.

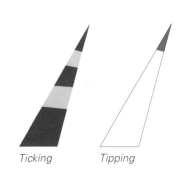

Ticking — *Tipping*

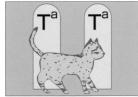

Aby (Agouti/Ticked) Tabby

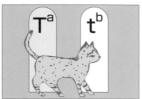

Aby (Agouti/Ticked) Tabby carrying the Mackerel Tabby Pattern

Aby (Agouti/Ticked) Tabby carrying the Classic Tabby Pattern

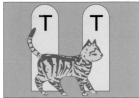

Mackerel Tabby Pattern

Mackerel Tabby Pattern carrying the Classic Tabby Pattern

Classic Tabby Pattern

Phenotypically (in their outward appearance) these cats may look like tabbies, but may be genetic solids. If the cat is highly rufoused and is a longhair, this pattern may not easily be seen.

Genotypically (in their genetic makeup), they may be either non-agouti or agouti. A rule of the thumb: if the red cat's chin is "whitish," the chances are the cat is a genetic tabby; if the chin is the same color as the rest of the body, the chances are it is a genetic solid.

All cats have tabby genes in their genotype, or genetic makeup. All tabbies have an "M" on the forehead and "pencil" markings on the face. There are three basic tabby patterns in the domestic feline, listed here in order of their dominance. The tabby pattern may be silvered or non-silvered.

Agouti Tabby

The agouti tabby (T^a) has the least amount of the tabby pattern in the Abyssinian and Somali Agouti tabby. This breed standard calls for no necklaces (or only broken, or unconnected, necklaces); no bracelets on the legs or belly spots; no tail rings; and a dorsal strip of color on the top of the tail, with the strip of color going around the end of the tail. There is never a tabby pattern of any kind on the torso. The torso should consist of ticked hairs only. In some cases this is referred to as the Agouti Tabby or the Aby Tabby.

When barring and necklaces are desired, many refer to this pattern as a Ticked Tabby.

Other breed standards, such as the Singapura, require barring on the inner front legs and on the back knees.

Mackerel Tabby

The mackerel tabby pattern (T) has head markings, leg bracelets, and dark color on the spine line, which has lines of the dark color extending down the sides of the cat. Rings on the tail tend to be rather narrow and close together.

Classic Tabby

The classic tabby pattern (t^b) has a "bull's-eye" on each side of the body, with a swirl of color surrounded by very bold, wide bands of the same color, with no lines going down the sides. This pattern is sometimes called a blotched tabby or "eggs on ham." The rings on the tail will usually be wider and farther apart.

Variations of Tabby Pattern

The spotted tabby appears to be the result of modifiers. These are a group of genes that work together to produce bodily characteristics; they change the effect of major genes,) breaking up the mackerel or the classic patterns into spots. If you look carefully at the spots, you can tell which pattern was broken.

The Bengal cat is the exception to this. The Bengal, which originated from the Asian Leopard Cat and a domestic cat, has spots and rosettes that are aligned horizontally, and the marbled pattern. The marbled pattern is similar to the classic pattern, but instead of circles, the pattern is more like a skewed rectangle.

Torbie

A torbie, also called a patched tabby or a tortie tabby, is a tortoiseshell cat turned tabby, with the introduction of the agouti gene. In the torbie, the patches of solid eumelanin color become tabby. The patches of phaeomelanin also show a tabby

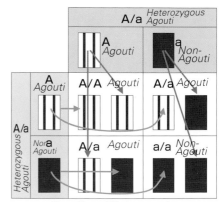

Breeding of Heterozygotes

pattern. The result is a glorious mixture of eumelanin tabby and phaeomelanin tabby flowing into each other and forming a complete tabby pattern. If you are in doubt if the cat is a tortie or a torbie, look in the eumelanistic areas. If these areas show a tabby pattern, the cat is a torbie; if there is no tabby pattern, the cat is a tortie. Also if the cat is a torbie, the belly should be spotted; without spots, the cat may be a tortie. Disregard the red or cream areas, as they will always show tabby pattern to a lesser or greater extent.

Torbies may be silvered, non-silvered, or golden; they may also be seen in the chinchilla or shaded silver/golden, and any of these patterns plus white spotting patterns.

Rufousing Polygenes

Polygenes are a group of smaller genes that influence the major genes. Rufousing polygenes affect the yellow bands and the ground color, changing the yellow band to an apricot- or burnt-orange-colored band and ground color. All tabbies have the rufousing polygenes. The smaller the number of these polygenes, the paler the bands and ground color will be, giving an almost dull beige color. The greater the number of the polygenes, the more intense the color will be. The rufousing

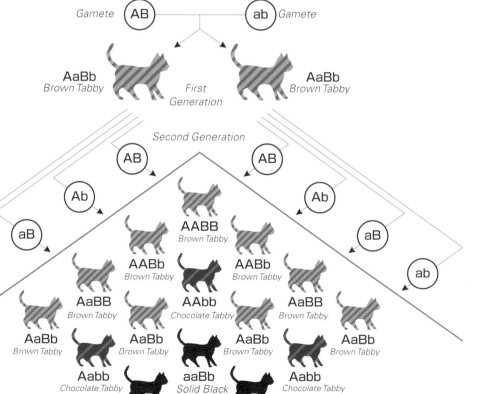

Atavism

The breeding between a homozygous dominant parent, Brown Tabby (AABB), and a homozygous recessive parent, Solid Chocolate (aabb), will produce heterozygous offspring, Brown Tabby (AaBb). From these heterozygous parents, four different gametes are produced, giving 16 different combinations in the second generation.

A = Agouti gene (Dominant to Non-Agouti)
a = Non-Agouti gene (Recessive to Agouti)
B = Black (Dominant to Chocolate)
b = Chocolate (Recessive to Black)

AABB *Brown Tabby* — **aabb** *Solid Chocolate*

Gamete **AB** — **ab** Gamete

AaBb *Brown Tabby* — First Generation — **AaBb** *Brown Tabby*

Second Generation

AB — **AB**
Ab — **Ab**
aB — **aB**
ab — **ab**

AABB *Brown Tabby*
AABb *Brown Tabby* — **AABb** *Brown Tabby*
AaBB *Brown Tabby* — **AAbb** *Chocolate Tabby* — **AaBB** *Brown Tabby*
AaBb *Brown Tabby* — **AaBb** *Brown Tabby* — **AaBb** *Brown Tabby* — **AaBb** *Brown Tabby*
Aabb *Chocolate Tabby* — **aaBb** *Solid Black* — **Aabb** *Chocolate Tabby*
aaBb *Solid Black* — **aaBb** *Solid Black*
aabb *Solid Chocolate*

polygenes also change the brown pattern on the torso to lighter shades of brown. This may be the result of rufousing polygenes being thermolabile (heat sensitive). The Abyssinian, Somali, and Bengal have a large quantity of these polygenes. While the

	X $\male$ Male	Y
X $\female$ Female	X/X $\female$ Female	X/Y $\male$ Male
X $\female$ Female	X/X $\female$ Female	X/Y $\male$ Male

Male and Female Punnet Square

cinnamon Abyssinian has a reddish appearance, especially in cats with a high degree of rufousing, it is not to be confused with the true red Abyssinian, which has the sex-linked red gene. If the sorrel were a true red, then a red bred to a ruddy would produce torbies. This does not happen.

Tortoiseshell

The tortoiseshell pattern is a mosaic of eumelanin and phaeomelanin patches of color. The tortie is a non-agouti cat, a solid-colored cat.

In the embryonic state, each female cell starts off with two active "X" chromosomes in its cells. If the cat is to be a tortie, she has received an X (Eumelanin) from one parent and an X^P (Phaeomelanin) from the other parent. Each cell may have only one X chromosome activated; therefore one X chromosome is inactivated at random. As these cells divide and multiply, patches of phaeomelanin or eumelanin develop, forming the tortoiseshell mosaic pattern over the cat's body. Breeders of Persian cats, however, report that they can selectively breed for the placement and the amount of pigment. An example of this is the "blaze," a distinct streak of the phaeomelanistic color that appears on the nose.

The tortie has been incorrectly described as having a three-color pattern: black, red, and cream. The "cream" areas may appear to be cream, but they are actually the ticked or banded hairs in the red tabby areas.

The tortie colors are black and red, chocolate and red, cinnamon and red, blue and cream, lilac and cream, and fawn and cream.

Tortoiseshell cats come in the traditional, sepia, pointed, and mink varieties.

Full Color Gene and Its Alleles

C = full color
c^b = sepia
c^s = pointed
c^a = blue-eyed white
c = albino

	Black Female $\female$	Red Female $\female$	Tortie Female $\female$
Black Male $\male$	$\male$ $\female$	$\male$ $\female$	$\male$ $\male$ $\female$ $\female$
Red Male $\male$	$\male$ $\female$	$\male$ $\female$	$\male$ $\male$ $\female$ $\female$

Breeding Chart

The full color gene (C) allows color to be fully developed. The color genes are black, chocolate, cinnamon, and red. The pigment synthesis is controlled by the heat-sensitive enzyme tyrosinase (Tyr) that resides at the C or Full Color Locus, also referred to as the Albino Locus.

If the dilution genes (d/d) are present: then black becomes blue; chocolate becomes lilac; cinnamon becomes fawn, and red becomes cream.

Examples of Full Color are any color that is not sepia, pointed, or mink. In TICA, we refer to these colors as the Traditional Colors, that is, any color that has not been altered by the c^b or c^s genes.

A full colored cat may carry sepia or pointed as a recessive gene; mink, however, cannot be carried.

Sepia, Pointed, and Mink Kittens

Pointed (c^s) kittens are born white. Note: In dealing with the (c^s) gene, it makes no difference what the basic color of the kittens is; they will still be born appearing to be white or colorless.

Sepia kittens may be born a pale tan color, while mink kittens may be born a coffee and cream color.

Tortoiseshell Formation

Cells form patches of Phaeomelanin and Eumelanin

The pointed kittens have been kept warm inside the mother's body prior to birth and therefore color development has not taken place. About 10 days following the birth, the coldest parts, i.e. the extremities (points), will develop the indicative color. You will see the color develop at the rims of the ears first. The torso is the warmest part of the body and will not develop the full intensity of the indicative color because the enzyme tyrosinase is heat sensitive. The torso and other warm areas of the body will be a light shade of the indicative color of the pointed areas.

Points

In the pointed, sepia, and mink, the indicative color is restricted to the extremities; these are referred to as points. In the pointed (c^s), the top and back of the head, neck, torso, and the legs will be a much lighter color, in some cases appearing to be an off white (especially in the red and creams). The feet will have color.

In the sepia and mink, the color of the top and back of the head, neck, torso, the legs, and feet will be only slightly lighter than the extremities. In viewing a seal sepia or seal mink, the cat may appear to be of one solid color all over. The points may be seen on the lighter colors. Black will be altered to seal brown color, for example.

Pointed Colors

To designate sepia, pointed, and mink, TICA uses the following terms: seal point, seal sepia, or seal mink; chocolate point, chocolate sepia, or chocolate mink; cinnamon point, cinnamon sepia, or cinnamon mink; blue point, blue sepia, or blue mink; lilac point, lilac sepia, or lilac mink; fawn point, fawn sepia, or fawn mink; red point (which is a beautiful tangerine color), red sepia, or red mink; and cream point, cream sepia, or cream mink.

Pointed Color Description

Seal should be a seal brown, chocolate should be the color of milk or dark chocolate, cinnamon should be the color of a cinnamon stick or cocoa powder, a blue should be a pale gray, a lilac should be a paler shade of the chocolate, and a fawn should be a paler shade of the cinnamon. As polygenes or modifiers work with the major color genes, there will be a wide range of colors.

The sepia, pointed, and mink may be seen in solid colors and in the tabby, tortie, and torbie patterns, silver tabby, chinchilla, or shaded silver/golden, smoke, and any of these colors and patterns plus the white spotting gene.

Sepia

Sepia refers to the old Burmese colors. The first mutation (c^b) at the C or full color locus changed eumelanin and phaeomelanin to sepia (c^b) color. The color gene is still in the genotype, but full color is not allowed to develop because the cat has the recessive c^b/c^b genes in the genotype instead of the dominant C. The c^b/c^b genes alter the color gene to the sepia colors listed above.

The genotype for a solid seal sepia shorthair is: a/a, B/-, c^b/c^b, D/-, i/i, L/-, s/s, T/-, wb/wb, w/w

The eye colors are gold or yellow, and green; the pigment in front of the eye is reduced, changing copper to gold or yellow. Copper eyes should not be possibile.

The enzyme tyrosinase in the sepia colors is not as heat sensitive as it is in the pointed (c^s) colors; therefore the torso and other warm areas develop a deeper color than that of a pointed (c^s) cat.

Pointed c^s

The genotype for a seal point shorthair is: a/a, B/-, c^s/c^s, D/-, i/i, L/-, s/s, T/-, wb/wb, w/w

GENES FOR COLOR AND PATTERN			
Dominant Genes		**Recessive Genes**	
symbol	name	symbol	name
A	Agouti	a/a	Non-agouti
B	Black	b/b	Chocolate Cinnamon
C	Full Color	c^b/c^b Sepia c^s/c^s Pointed c^b/c^s Mink	
D	Dense Pigmentation	d/d	Dilution
I	Inhibitor	I/i	Non-inhibitor Gene
P^{van}	High degree of spotting pattern	$P^{bi-color}$ Bicolor P^{mitted} Mitted	
S	White Spotting Factor	s/s	No white spotting
T^a	Ticked or Agouti Tabby Pattern	T Mackerel Tabby t^b/t^b Classic Tabby	
W	Dominant White	w/w	No white
Wb	Wide Band	wb/wb	No wide band

GENETIC SYMBOLS FOR BODY PARTS			
Dominant Genes		**Recessive Genes**	
symbol	name	symbol	name
Ac	Curled back ears	ac	Normal ears
Jb	Normal tail length	jb	Japanese Bobtail-like tail
M	Manx-like tail or tailless	m	Normal tail length
Pd	Polydactyl	pd	Normal number of toes
Sf	Folded down ears	sf	Normal ears

GENETIC SYMBOLS FOR HAIR			
Dominant Genes		**Recessive Genes**	
symbol	name	symbol	name
Hr	Normal hair	hr/hr	Hairless
L	Short hair	l/l	Long hair
Lp	La Perm	lp/lp	No Rex coat
R	Normal coat	r/r Cornish Rex coat re/re Devon Rex coat	
Sr	Selkirk Rex coat	sr/sr	No Selkirk Rex coat
Wh	Wirehair coat	wh/wh	No Wirehair coat

SOLID COLOR GENOTYPES			
Full Color	Sepia	Pointed	Mink
Black (a/a, B/-, C/-, D/-)	Seal Sepia (a/a, B/-, c^b, c^b, D/-)	Seal Point (a/a, B/-, c^s, c^s, D/-)	Seal Mink (a/a, B/-, c^b/c^s, D/-)
Blue (a/a, B/-, C/-, d/d-)	Blue Sepia (a/a, B/-, c^b/c^b, d/d)	Blue Point (a/a, B/-, c^s/c^s, d/d)	Blue Mink (a/a, B/-, c^b/c^s, d/d)
Chocolate (a/a, b/b, C/-, D/-)	Chocolate Sepia (a/a, b/b, c^b/c^b, D/-)	Chocolate Point (a/a, b/b, c^s/c^s, D/-)	Chocolate Mink (a/a, b/b, c^b/c^s, D/-)
Lilac (a/a, b/b, C/-, D/-)	Lilac Sepia (a/a, b/b, c^b/c^b, d/d)	Lilac Point (a/a, b^1/b^1, c^s/c^s, D/-)	Lilac Mink (a/a, b/b, c^b/c^s, d/d)
Cinnamon (a/a, b^1/b^1, C/-, D/-)	Cinnamon Sepia (a/a, b^1/b^1, c^b/c^b, D/-)	Cinnamon Point (a/a, b^1/b^1, c^s/c^s, D/-)	Cinnamon Mink (a/a, b^1/b^1, c^b/c^s, D/-)
Fawn (a/a, b^1/b^1, C/-, d/d)	Fawn Sepia (a/a, b^1/b^1, c^b/c^b, d/d)	Fawn Point (a/a, b^1/b^1, c^s/c^s, D/-)	Fawn Mink (a/a, b^1/b^1, c^b, c^s, d/d)
Red (B/-, C/-, D/-)	Red Sepia (B/-, c^b/c^b, D/-)	Red Point (B/-, c^s/c^s, D/-)	Red Mink (B/-, c^b/c^s, D/-)
Cream (B/-, C/-, d/d)	Cream Sepia (B/-, c^b/c^b, d/d)	Cream Point (B/-, c^s/c^s, d/d)	Cream Mink (B/-, c^b/c^s, d/d)

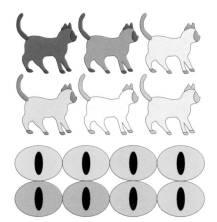

Eye Color and Hair Color of Sepia

Pointed refers to the old Siamese colors. The extremities or points will have the indicative color development, while in most cases, the warmer parts of the body will be many shades lighter than the color of the points. In the lighter colors, the warm areas may be almost white in appearance. All (c^s) pointed cats will have blue eyes because there is no pigment in the front of the iris.

In reference to the tabby points, we refer to them as Lynx Points. Hint: If in doubt of the color of a Lynx Point, look at the tip of the tail as this will give you more information concerning the indicative color, because there is more hair at the tip of the tail than on the ears or in the tabby pattern, therefore more color. Many times, as a pointed (c^s) cat grows older, the circulation is not good, and the torso may become very dark in color. This dark color is not to be confused with sepia or mink.

Mink c^b/c^s

The genotype for a seal mink shorthair is: a/a, B/-, c^b/c^s, D/-, i/i, L/-, s/s, T/-, wb/wb, w/w

Mink refers to the old Tonkinese colors.

Mink (c^b/c^s) is a blending of sepia and pointed and therefore cannot be considered an allele. In order to produce a mink, a pointed must be bred to a sepia. This is an example of co-dominance.

The mink cat closely resembles the sepia cat, except that the points

are more visible due to the body color being a shade lighter than the point color. The body color is not as dark as the sepia's and not as light as the pointed.

The eye color may be the only helping factor to determine whether the cat is a sepia or a mink–if it is a washed-out aqua, then the chances are it is a mink. The eye color of the mink ranges from green-blue to blue-green; there will always be more blue than green-yellow.

Last two mutations at the Full Color Locus

c^a = blue-eyed white
c = albino

It is easy to confuse this form of blue-eyed white with the blue eyes of a Dominant White or a Piebald White Spotted cat. This form of blue-eyed white is very rare, as are true albino cats.

Dense Pigmentation and Dilute Pigmentation

D = dense pigmentation
d/d = dilute pigmentation

With dense pigmentation (D/D or D/d), the pigment granules are deposited in a uniform manner along the hair shaft. Light is reflected off the entire surface, giving a darker color.

With dilute pigmentation (d/d),

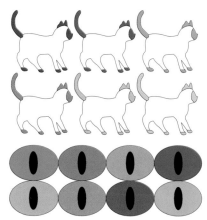

Eye Color and Hair Color of Pointed

also called maltesing, the granules are deposited in clusters (like clusters of grapes) in the hair shaft, allowing less light reflection, resulting in a lighter color. Any of the densely pigmented

phaeomelanistic or eumelanistic colors may be maltesed.

Black diluted = blue, chocolate diluted = lilac, cinnamon diluted = fawn, red diluted = cream

Inhibitor Gene (Silver)

I = inhibitor of pigment
i = no inhibition of pigment

The inhibitor gene (I/-), sometimes called the silver gene, is responsible

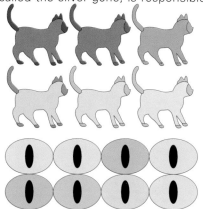

Eye Color and Hair Color of Mink

for the silver color found on silver tabbies, chinchilla and shaded silvers, and smoke solids.

Silver is the result of a lack of pigment granules in the hair shaft. The pigment is inhibited, so no yellow banding or ground color is present.

The recessive of the inhibitor gene is (i/i). If (i/i) is in the genotype, pigment will be produced.

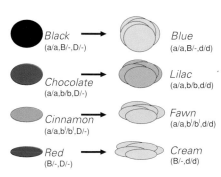

Dense and Dilute Colors

Black (a/a,B/-,D/-) → Blue (a/a,B/-,d/d)

Chocolate (a/a,b/b,D/-) → Lilac (a/a,b/b,d/d)

Cinnamon (a/a,b^l/b^l,D/-) → Fawn (a/a,b^l/b^l,d/d)

Red (B/-,D/-) → Cream (B/-,d/d)

20

The silver gene appears to operate only on the shredded or weakened phaeomelanin granules found on agouti hairs (bands of yellow and the ground color), making it possible for red or cream silver tabbies to be produced. We do not know much about the Inhibitor gene. It is possible that it works on any weakened melanin, which would help explain a Smoke.

Silver Tabbies *A/-, I/-, T/-, w^b/w^b*

The silver tabby pattern is thoroughly established in the American Shorthair silver classic tabby (T, I/-, w^b/w^b [the recessive of the "wide band" gene]). The pattern is a striking contrast of black and silver swirls; when the hair is parted, a silvery white ground color can be seen. Tarnishing, which occurs when the inhibitor does not completely inhibit the production of yellow in the hair, may be seen on the muzzle, the edges of the feet, and the hocks (back feet). Breeders have selectively bred to eliminate this tarnishing from the gene pool. Rufousing polygenes can be so powerful that it may take four or five generations before the tarnish disappears.

Any of the tabby patterns, including the torbie, may be silvered.

Shaded

Chinchilla and Shaded Silver
A/-, I/-, T/-, Wb/-

The chinchilla and shaded cats are essentially tabby cats with the inhibitor gene and dominant "wide band" gene (the gene responsible for the wide band or tip of color on the hair) added. These cats have "tipped" hairs. In the chinchilla, only the tip of each guard hair has pigment. In the shaded, almost half of the hair, from the tip down, has pigment. The undercoat (the pigmentless portion of the hairs) is silvered. A chinchilla cat will appear to be almost white; just the tips of the guard hairs show color. A shaded cat will appear to have a mantle of color thrown over its back; shadeds are born with either the mackerel or classic tabby pattern showing. Most chinchilla or shaded cats will have green eyes;

Chinchilla | Shaded
Smoke
Tipped Hairs

however, many do not and will have yellow to gold eye color.

Chinchilla and Shaded Golden and Golden Tabbies
A/-, i/i, T/-, Wb/- = chinchilla or shaded golden
A/-. i/i, T/-, w^b/w^b = golden tabby

A chinchilla or shaded golden is the same as the chinchilla or shaded silver, except the Inhibitor gene is not active. A chinchilla or shaded golden should be highly rufoused, the wide band displaying an almost burnt orange color. Also please note that modifiers may be present to alter the width of the wide band.

There are many differences of opinion as to the gene that is responsible for the golden color. Peter Prose (now deceased) once said Golden was a dominant major gene.

Mr. Prose was a famous feline geneticist who lived in the Netherlands. He has published several books on Feline Color Genetics, including *Practical Cat Genetics for the Breeders of Persian Cats* by P.J. Prose. 1989. Copyright Edition by J.D. Lambrechts, Belgium.

Others, myself included, believe the golden gene and the rufousing polygenes are the same. Still others hold that the terms *chinchilla golden* and *shaded golden* are reserved strictly for Persians. However, if chin-

chilla and shaded silvers are possible in other cat breeds, then why would the same principle not apply to other breeds? The Abyssinian, Somali, and Bengal may be considered to be golden tabbies.

Smoke *a/a, I/-, w^b/w^b*

Smokes are non-agouti, non-tabby cats, with the inhibitor (silver) gene. In the smoke, three-quarters of the hair has pigment, which may be a result of the inhibitor gene that suppresses pigment formation in the portion of the hair that is grown last. The smoke is a solid cat, with no yellow bands on the hair shaft.

The smoke cat appears to have solid-color hairs until the cat moves and the hairs are parted, revealing a white undercoat. However, the undercoat of the smoke cat is not a sparkling white; the color is off-white, leaning sometimes toward the pale gray tones. To determine whether a cat is a smoke, part the hair at the top of the head. If there is no white (or off-white) undercoat showing, the cat may not be a smoke. Young smokes may display a tabby pattern, which usually disappears with age.

Please note, there may be another gene involved here that eliminates the pigment in the hairs near the skin in the solid-colored cat. We know that the Inhibitor is there because when we breed a smoke X brown tabby (for example) we get silver tabbies. There is still very much that we do not understand about the silver or the gene(s) that cause a solid-colored cat to be smoked.

White

White is the absence of color. White hairs are caused when melanoblasts which turn into melanocytes, or pigment-producing cells) do not migrate from their point of origin to the hair shaft. This occurs in cats that have the white spotting gene or the dominant white gene; in these cats migration of the melanoblasts is partially or completely stopped. The absence of melanocytes causes an absence of pigment. If there is no pigment, the hair shaft is empty, and the hair is white.

Likewise, if the melanocytes do not reach the front of the iris in the eye, the eye has no color. In the absence of melanocytes, the eyes appear blue. A chance of deafness accompanies blue-eyed whites (dominant white and piebald white spotting). However, not all blue-eyed cats are deaf. If the color being masked in the white cat is the pointed color, the eyes will be blue but the chances of deafness occurring are very slim. If the eye is colored, and not blue, most likely melanocytes have marched down to give the eye color; it is likely that a white cat with colored eyes will not be deaf. If the cat has one copper eye and one blue eye, the ear on the blue-eyed side may be deaf.

If melanocytes do not reach the ear, the ear canal remains closed. With the closing of the ear, the cochlea does not receive a supply of blood, and it degenerates. The nerve cells of the cochlea then die and permanent deafness results. The exact cause of this vascular degeneration is not known, but it appears to be associated with the absence of melanocytes in the blood vessels.

Dominant White

W = dominant white

w = dominant white is not operative

White is not a color, but the absence of color, the masking of all colors and patterns. Color and pattern genes may

be present in the genotype but may not be expressed if dominant white. These color or patterns are said to be masked. (W/-) is present. If the cells have one or more copies of the dominant white gene, most melanoblasts do not migrate at all, except to the eyes and hopefully to the ears.

Dominant white kittens may have a "kitten cap," or a patch of color on the top of the head. This patch of color will tell the breeder what color is being masked; the color usually disappears by the time the cat is 18 months of age. This patch of color should not be confused with the patch of color that may appear in kittens with the Van pattern; the spot of color that is due to the dominant white gene will go away with age, but the color that is due to the white spotting gene in the Van pattern will not go away.

Breeding dominant whites together is like opening Pandora's box. If both parents are heterozygous (W/w), a full spectrum of color and patterns could appear in the kittens. However, some of the dominant white Persians will only produce dominant whites, especially if they have been bred dominant white to dominant white for a long time; the chances

are that the white parents are each homozygous for this trait.

Piebald White Spotting

S = Piebald White spotting gene

s = the Piebald White spotting gene is not operative

In TICA all cats displaying Piebald White Spotting are judged in the Particolor Division.

The white spotting gene (S) is responsible for white accompanied by color and/or patterns. It is a dominant gene that may be an incomplete dominance in the heterozygous form (S/s).

White spotting is recognized in four main patterns: mitted, bicolor, harlequin, and Van. There are many sub-patterns and polygenes at work, however, giving a great deal of variation to the patterns. White spotting can range from just one white toe to white on the body to the body being completely white with just a spot of color on the head. It is likely that there is more than one white spotting gene, as there is in mice, horses, and other animals.

The exact placement and amount of white is extremely difficult to control. In breeds like the Birman that have been bred Birman to Birman for

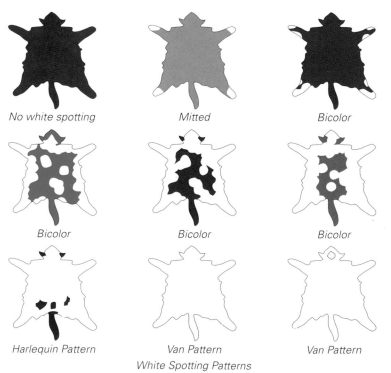

No white spotting   *Mitted*   *Bicolor*

Bicolor   *Bicolor*   *Bicolor*

Harlequin Pattern   *Van Pattern*   *Van Pattern*

White Spotting Patterns

White spotting patterns vary greatly, depending on the pattern. The lowest level of spotting could simply be a few white hairs on the toes, or white feet (white feet are referred to as the mitted pattern). The middle level is seen in the bicolor, and the highest level in the van.

so many years, many of he breeders have obtained the desired White Gloving pattern.

Numerous theories exist regarding the cause of white spotting. It is believed that if the cells contain one or two copies of the white spotting gene, the melanocytes may begin to migrate from the neural crest (an area at the top of the embryo where melanocytes and other cells are formed) but some fail to survive. It is also possible that, just as the agouti gene is necessary to bring forth the tabby pattern in the genotype, the white spotting gene must be present for the colored areas to become active.

A theory I hold true is that cats do have pattern genes for the colored areas. It takes the presence of the White Spotting gene to bring forth this pattern. If there is no White Spotting gene (and it is a dominant gene), there is no visual pattern, but the gene remains in the genotype.

The gene that causes white lockets, small areas that are different from the desired color, may be the result of an entirely separate white spotting gene. It appears to be a recessive gene, as the white spot stays in one place (upper chest or groin area) and does not necessarily grow larger.

A note about the torties and white. In some organizations they are called Calicos, while in other organizations, they might be called Particolors. In TICA, they are called simply tortie and white, blue tortie and white, chocolate tortie and white, etc. The cats are not judged based on the amount or placement of the white (except in the Birman, Ragdoll, and Snowshoe), as it is understood that this exact placement and amount of white is very difficult to control. Instead the cat is judged on how its type meets the standard.

Blood Type

Note: The markers on the blood cells in the domestic cat are not the same as those in humans. Therefore the reagents for testing feline blood are not that same as those used in testing human blood. The A and B blood types *in cats are not the same as the ABO blood type systems in humans. Using capital letter symbols would indicate that A is dominant and B is dominant. This is fine in referring to human blood type, as A/B can be co-dominant. In domestic cats, this is not true as this is a dominant and a recessive situation. To be more explicit, the genes for blood type are alleles and not two separate genes at different loci A and B.*

So as not to confuse the reader, the traditional accepted symbols of A and B will be used, yet I insert my own symbols so we can see the blood groups as homozygous or heterozygous. I am going to use the symbol G for the dominant and g for the recessive.

In all breeds of cats type B (g) is recessive to type A (G); in the homozygous (G/G or g/g); in the heterozygous (G/g). It is very important to understand that the blood type may be heterozygous, which will explain why when a G/g is bred to a G/g, some of the kittens will be all right and some may die. O blood type, to the best of my knowledge, does not exist in cats.

Studies of blood type in pedigreed cats have shown that the frequency of type B (g) blood varies greatly; some have no known type B (g) at all. The recessive blood type appears to be rare. The Siamese, Burmese, and Oriental Shorthairs that were tested have type A blood.

If a cat with B (g/g) blood type were given a transfusion of A (G/G) blood type, it would be fatal to the B (g/g) blood type cat. For this reason, it is important that breeders and cat owners know the blood type of their cat.

Another reason it is important to be aware of cats' blood types is that a breeding between an A (G/G) blood type male and a B (g/g) blood type female may result in Neonatal Erythrolysis in the resulting kittens.

Now is a good time to explain why, in the domestic cat, we are NOT dealing with two dominant genes (A and B). If both parents are homozygous for the same blood type, there is no problem. If the sire is heterozygous and is of type A (G/g in my book), some of the kittens will be in trouble. In the fourth and fifth charts, the Dams have very strong antibodies against type A (G). Therefore, type A (G) kittens born to a type B (g/g) dam are in trouble, while the B/B (g/g) are not in trouble.

As A (G) has a weak reaction to B (g), none of these kittens should have problems.

A and B Blood Types

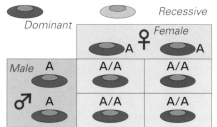

Kittens are all A/A. No problem.

Kittens are all B/B. No problem.

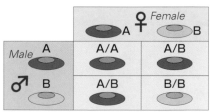

This is a heterozygous queen bred to a heterozygous sire; both are A blood type. As A blood type has a weak reaction to the antigens in B/B blood type, none of these kittens should be at risk.

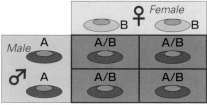

Kittens with A blood type are in trouble: the dam's type antibodies will attack the A type antigens.

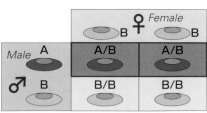

The A/B kittens are in trouble. The B/B kittens are not at risk.

Neonatal Erythrolysis (hemolysis of the newborn) has recently been recognized as a major cause of death in newborn kittens. Under certain conditions, the maternal antibodies in the colostrom (mother's first milk) actually destroy the kittens' red blood cells. Kittens are born healthy; the symptoms usually appear within hours after the kittens begin to nurse. In all feline mothers, the maternal antibodies pass into the milk for a day or two after birth, giving the kittens immediate passive immunity. Type B (g/g) mothers have very strong antibodies against type A (G/G). If the kittens have type A (G/G) blood, their red blood cells may be destroyed by the antibodies in the mother's colostrom. A kitten affected by this condition will stop nursing; it will deteriorate and look weak; its urine will be red or brown; it may be anemic or jaundiced; and it may die.

The condition may be treated by having the kittens stop nursing from their mother for 24 to 48 hours. Recent studies indicate that the kittens are only able to absorb antibodies for 18 hours, but some researchers have come up with different lengths of time. A cessation of 48 hours should be sufficient. A surrogate feline mother who is of the right blood type might be able to nurse the kittens, or the owner could tube-feed the babies, for 48 hours or until the danger has passed. (Pedialyte may be preferable over milk substitutes, since kittens may not be

	♀ q Female	q
♂ Male Q	Q/q	Q/q
Q	Q/q	Q/q

able to metabolize the milk right away.) When the colostrum is no longer being produced by the mother, the kittens may be returned to her.

Immune System

The key to understanding the feline immune system is the knowledge

	♀ Q Female	q
♂ Male Q	Q/Q	Q/q
q	Q/q	q/q

that the immune system genes are inherited.

A kitten receives immune system genes from each parent. The more diversity in the pedigree, the more diversity in the genes; the better the immune system. When parents and grandparents appear many, many times in a pedigree, the immune genes will be inherited from these parents and grandparents. It is not a good practice to continuously in-breed (related parents) or line breed (stay within the same "blood" line). This practice could jeopardize the immune system of the offspring. If these breeding techniques are continued over many generations, the whole cattery could be wiped out by a disease.

The immune system is probably the most complicated body system of all and it is certainly unique. It can shuffle its genes when needed to fight off a disease.

The cat's first defense against a disease is the skin. If an antigen gets past the skin, and into the body, then the defense system must take over. The defense system is made up of white blood cells that are produced in the bone marrow. These cells are the "killer" cells and are absolutely essential to the immune system. One of the killer cells is called a T-Cell. The T-Cells, like the B-Cells (that produce antibodies), have receptors. A receptor is like a lock and key, and is specific for one and only one antigen.

Memory Cells and Antibodies

The immune system has wonderful, wonderful cells called Memory Cells.

When an antigen (foreign body) is introduced into the body, be it a virus or bacterium, the immune system makes Memory Cells (if they have not already been made and are sleeping). These cells produce antibodies against this specific antigen. The antibodies then hold the antigen in place until a killer cell can destroy them. Once the antigens have been destroyed, these particular Memory Cells "go to sleep", as they are no longer needed. They will, however, wake up and produce antibodies if that particular antigen appears again.

If the cat is exposed to a disease and there are no Memory Cells for that specific antigen, the immune system must call upon the genes (that are hopefully already there) to make the memory cells that will produce the antibodies. This usually takes about seven days. During that time, the cat may be very, very sick and if already weakened, could die before antibodies can be produced. Good nursing and gentle care are key to keeping the cat alive during this precarious stretch of time.

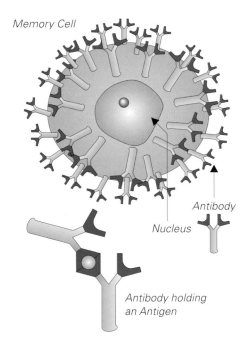

Memory Cell

Antibody

Nucleus

Antibody holding an Antigen

Signs of a Weakened Immune System
- Low fertiltiy
- The cats are getting smaller in size in subsequent breeds
- The number of kittens in the litters decreasing
- Regular occurence of cancer in young cats
- Death of cats or kittens to one specific disease

Vaccines

Vaccines are used to trick antibody production against a specific antigen. Live vaccines will give the cat a mild dose of the virus, not enough to kill the animal, but enough to cause Memory Cells to be produced. Live vaccines may be risky and, in my opinion, should never be used on young kittens. A killed vaccine is better, in that it does trick the body into producing Memory Cells without actually causing the animal to come down with the disease. Please check with your vet for the latest information on vaccines.

Some final words on genetics

Remember that recessive genes may be hidden or lurking in the heritage for generation after generation. It takes two recessive genes coming together in order for the trait to be expressed. Test breeding to try to find and get rid of recessive genes is almost impossible.

Breeders should be extremely careful about in-breeding and line breeding. Occasionally it is necessary to achieve a desirable trait or to see some of the traits the cats may be carrying, but it should always be done with caution and knowledge. Too much in-breeding, and you may produce cats that are susceptible to diseases for which they have no immunity.

Certain breeds have inherited disorders that can be lethal to the cat. Breeders should be aware of this and breed with caution, and should always know as much as possible about the genetic background of the cats that are to be bred.

It is easy to get caught up with the idea of breeding for specific color and pattern, but genetic diversity should be the first and foremost concern, and color and pattern always secondary.

There are certain breeders and organizations that believe in the idea of a "pure bred" cat. It's close to impossible to find such a cat. For instance, many breeds have the Siamese or the pointed gene in their background.

Variances within a litter of color and attributes should not be a cause of concern.

TICA has a broad knowledge of genetics, and in judging shows allows, for example, a longhaired cat from two Exotic Shorthairs to be shown as a Persian; pointed cats out of Orientals to be shown as Siamese; sable-colored cats from Bombays to be shown as Burmese. The judges' books do not supply genetic information about the cats. The pedigrees are as genetically accurate as the information that the breeders put into the pedigree.

We in the Cat Fancy are honor bound to produce healthy cats. All of the points won at a cat show mean nothing if a cat is unhealthy.

Body Type Chart

Oriental

Cornish Rex

Siamese

Foreign

Somali

Abyssinian

Japanese Bobtail

Semi-Foreign

Devon Rex

Havana

American Curl

American Curl Shorthair

Egyptian Mau

La Perm

Semi-Cobby

Bombay

Chartreux

American Shorthair

American Wirehair

British Shorthair

Cobby

Burmese

Manx

Cymric

Substantial

Bengal

Birman

Maine Coon

Norwegian Forest Cat

This chart classifies the breeds introduced in this book into six body types. The long and slim type is Oriental on one end and the short and round Cobby on the other end. In between are Foreign, Semi-Foreign, and Semi-Cobby as the roundness increases. The large and substantial type, which does not fit in any of these types, is Substantial. Substantial can be subclassified, and it is briefly explained in the pages of each breed in this classification. It is the purpose of this chart to cover all the breeds in this book and to provide an overall view of body types.

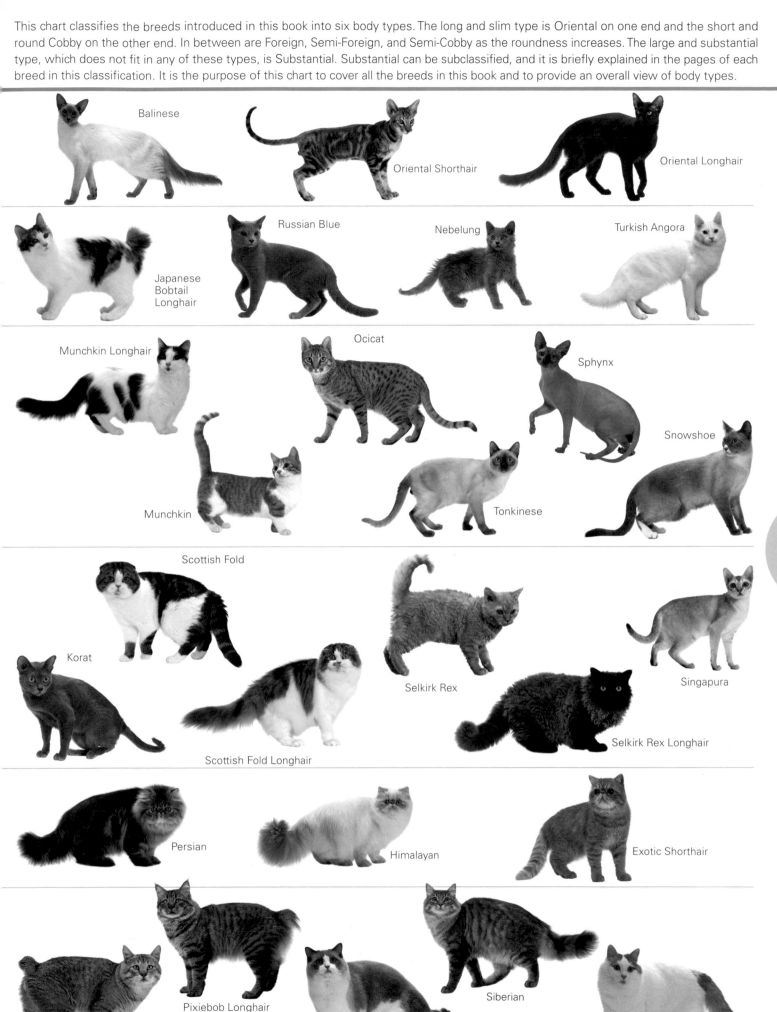

Balinese

Oriental Shorthair

Oriental Longhair

Japanese Bobtail Longhair

Russian Blue

Nebelung

Turkish Angora

Munchkin Longhair

Ocicat

Sphynx

Munchkin

Tonkinese

Snowshoe

Scottish Fold

Korat

Scottish Fold Longhair

Selkirk Rex

Selkirk Rex Longhair

Singapura

Persian

Himalayan

Exotic Shorthair

Pixiebob Longhair

Pixiebob

Ragdoll

Siberian

Turkish Van

Solid

Black

Chocolate

Blue

Lilac

Tortoiseshell

Tortoiseshell

Chocolate Tortie

Blue Tortie

Brown Agouti Tabby (Rudi)

Brown Classic Tabby

Seal Sepia Spotted Tabby

Chocolate Classic Tabby

Brown Marbled Tabby

Seal Mink Spotted Tabby

Chocolate Mackerel Tabby

Sable Ticked Tabby

Brown Mackerel Tabby

Brown Classic Torbie

Chocolate Spotted Tabby

Seal Classic Tabby

Tabby *Brown Ticked Tabby*

Seal Mink Classic Tabby

Brown Spotted Tabby

Brown Mackerel Torbie

Chocolate Mackerel Torbie

Tipped

Chinchilla Silver

Shaded Silver

Black Smoke

Tortie Smoke

Silver Agouti Tabby (Silver)

Silver Mackerel Tabby

Silver Classic Torbie

Silver Spotted

Silver Classic Tabby

Silver Spotted Tabby

Cinnamon Silver Agouti Tabby

Silver

Silver Mackerel Torbie

Cinnamon Silver Spotted Tabby

Seal Point

Seal Sepia (Sable)

Chocolate Point

Cinnamon Lynx Point

Chocolate Lynx Point

Chocolate Sepia

Seal Lynx Point

Chocolate (Champagne) Mink

Pointed

Seal Tortie Point

Seal (Natural) Mink

Chocolate Tortie Point

Cinnamon Tortie Point

28

Cats' coat colors and patterns are tremendously varied. All this is due to the work of genes in chromosomes. Taking the genes' operation into consideration, this chart classifies the coat colors and patterns into six types: Solid, Tortoiseshell, Tabby, Tipped, Silver, and Pointed. It also tries to give as many examples as possible. White is not a color; it is classifed as Solid only for convenience's sake. For the genetic reason, Torbie is classified as Tabby and Sepia and Mink as Pointed.

Fawn

Red

Cream

White

Seal Sepia Tortie

Cinnamon Agouti Tabby (Sorrel)

Blue Classic Tabby

Red Classic Tabby

Lilac Spotted Tabby

Cream Classic Tabby

Cinnamon Spotted Tabby

Blue Mackerel Tabby

Fawn Agouti Tabby (Fawn)

Red Mackerel Tabby

Cream Mackerel Tabby

Blue Ticked Tabby

Blue Agouti Tabby (Blue)

Blue Spotted Tabby

Fawn Spotted Tabby

Red Spotted Tabby

Cream Spotted Tabby

Chinchilla Golden

Shaded Golden

Blue Smoke

Red Shaded

Red Smoke

Blue Silver Classic Tabby

Blue Silver Agouti Tabby

Blue Silver Mackerel Tabby

Lilac Silver Spotted Tabby

Blue Silver Spotted Tabby

Red Silver Classic Tabby

Red Silver Mackeral Tabby

Cream Silver Classic Tabby

Blue Point

Blue Sepia

Lilac Sepia

Red Sepia

Blue Mink

Lilac (Platinum) Mink

Fawn Sepia

Blue Lynx Point

Lilac Point

Red Point

Cream Point

29

Color & Pattern Chart ②

Solid & White

Black & White

Blue & White

Chocolate & White

Tortoiseshell & White

Tortoiseshell & White

Chocolate Tortie & White

Tabby & White

Brown Ticked Tabby & White

Brown Spotted Tabby & White

Brown Classic Torbie & White

Brown Spotted Torbie & White

Brown Classic Tabby & White

Brown Mackerel Tabby & White

Brown Mackerel Torbie & White

Chocolate Classic Tabby & White

Tipped & White

Smoke Tortie & White

Black Smoke & White

Silver & White

Silver Classic Tabby & White

Silver Mackerel Tabby & White

Pointed & White

Seal Point Mitted

Seal Tortie Point & White

Chocolate Point Bi-color

Seal Tortie Point Mitted

Seal Point & White

Seal Lynx Point Mitted

Chocolate Point Mitted

Seal Point Bi-color

Chocolate Tortie Point & White

This chart shows six more types, which have White in addition to the six colors and patterns in Chart 1.

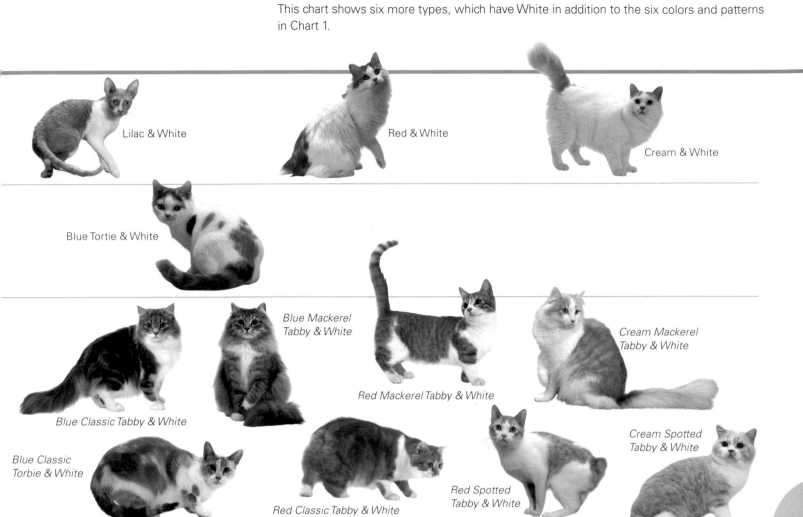

Lilac & White

Red & White

Cream & White

Blue Tortie & White

Blue Classic Tabby & White

Blue Mackerel Tabby & White

Red Mackerel Tabby & White

Cream Mackerel Tabby & White

Blue Classic Torbie & White

Red Classic Tabby & White

Red Spotted Tabby & White

Cream Spotted Tabby & White

Silver Classic Torbie & White

Cream Silver Classic Tabby & White

Blue Point & White

Cream Lynx Point Mitted

Blue Tortie Point & White

Blue Point Mitted

Red Lynx Point Mitted

Blue Lynx Point Mitted

Blue Point Bi-color

Lilac Point Mitted

Cream Point Mitted

Lilac Point Bicolor

Head Shape Chart

ROUND

Persian

Himalayan

Scottish Fold Longhair

Cymric

Birman

Exotic Shorthair

American Shorthair

Scottish Fold

Manx

Selkirk Rex Longhair

Bombay

Burmese

Selkirk Rex

Pixiebob

Munchkin

American Wirehair

British Shorthair

Singapura

Ocicat

Bengal

Chartreux

Snowshoe

Tonkinese

Havana

Sphynx

SHORTHAIR

Just like body types, cats' head shapes vary greatly. This chart tries to give an overall view of head shapes as viewed from front. The Persian on the top left corner and the Siamese on the bottom right corner represent the most round shape and the most pointy shape respectively. In between are shown other shapes as they gradually change the roundness. On the upper side of an imaginary diagonal line between the Persian and the Siamese are longhaired breeds and on the lower side shorthaired breeds.

LONGHAIR

Maine Coon

Turkish Van

Ragdoll

Siberian

Norwegian Forest Cat

Pixiebob Longhair

Munchkin Longhair

Somali

La Perm

Nebelung

Abyssinian

American Curl Shorthair

American Curl

Japanese Bobtail Longhair

Turkish Angora

Egyptian Mau

Japanese Bobtail

Cornish Rex

Oriental Longhair

Balinese

Devon Rex

Korat

Russian Blue

Oriental Shorthair

Siamese

WEDGE

Eye Color Chart

Eye color is determined in the smooth muscle cells of the iris, which is a small disk around the pupil or, maybe, the other way around; the pupil is a hole in the iris. Without pigment in the iris, it would look like a tiny, transparent doughnut.

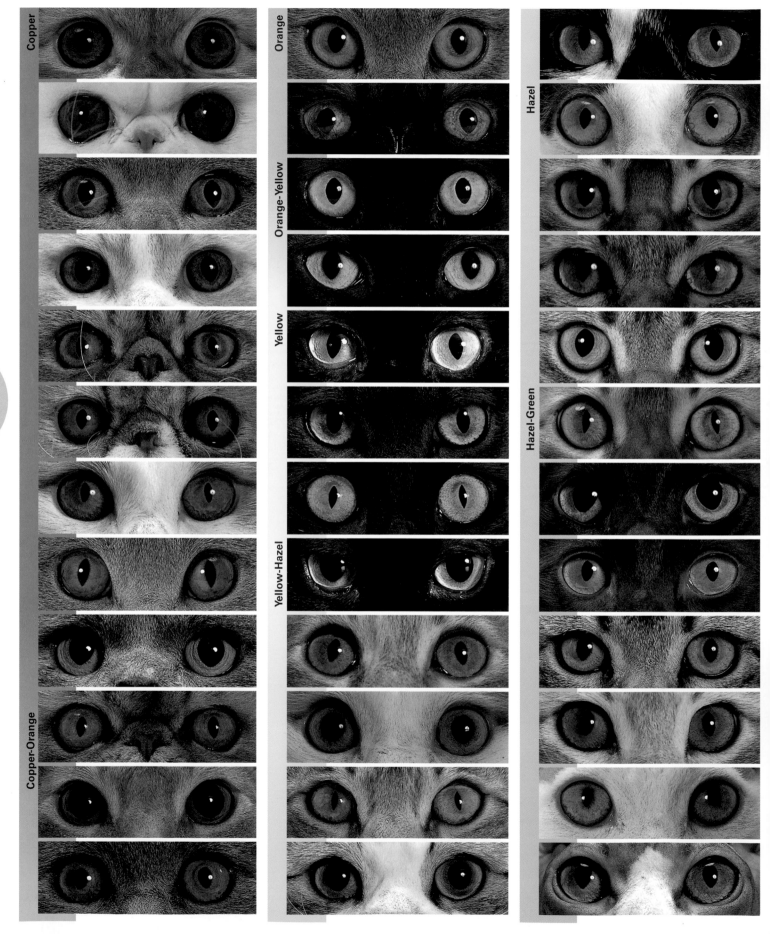

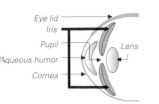

Eye lid
Iris
Pupil
Aqueous humor
Cornea
Lens

The iris has two halves, a front half (facing out) and a rear half. It is the amount of pigment that is deposited in the front and in the rear of the iris (in some cases separately) that determines the intensity of the color.

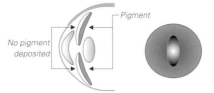

Pigment

No pigment deposited

Blue eye color is the result of an optical effect. There is no pigment in the front layer of the iris; there is pigment in the rear of the iris. The light rays go in, and are reflected back blue. The amount of eumelanin in the rear layer will determine the depth of the blue.

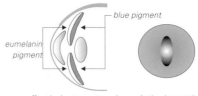

blue pigment

eumelanin pigment

The green effect is due to scattered eumelanin pigment in front of the iris acting with the blue reflection (yellow + blue = green). Green eye color varies according to the amount of pigment in the front and in the rear of the iris.

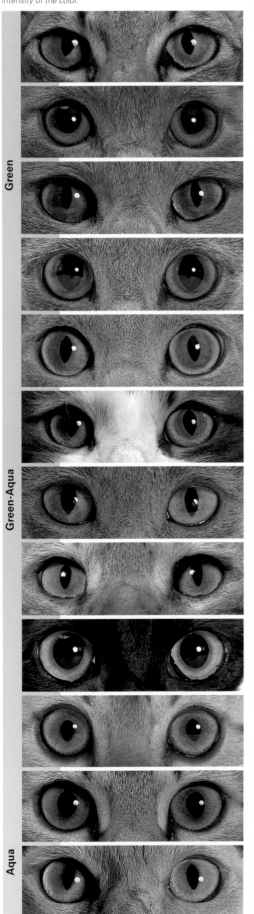

Green

Green-Aqua

Aqua

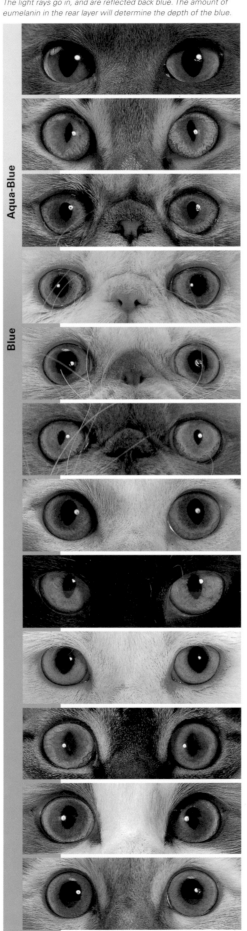

Aqua-Blue

Blue

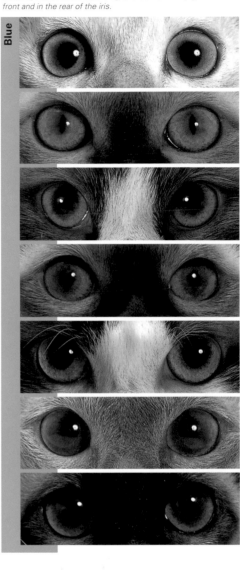

Blue

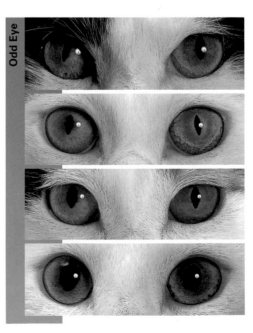

Odd Eye

How to Use the Profiles of Cats

Breed Name

When there are two or more breed names, it means that they share the same body type.

Eye Color Codes

Eye colors that are recognized are shown in full color and the eye colors that are not recognized are shown in gray for each breed in the codes. The note under the color codes distinguishes if the eye color has any relationship with the coat color.

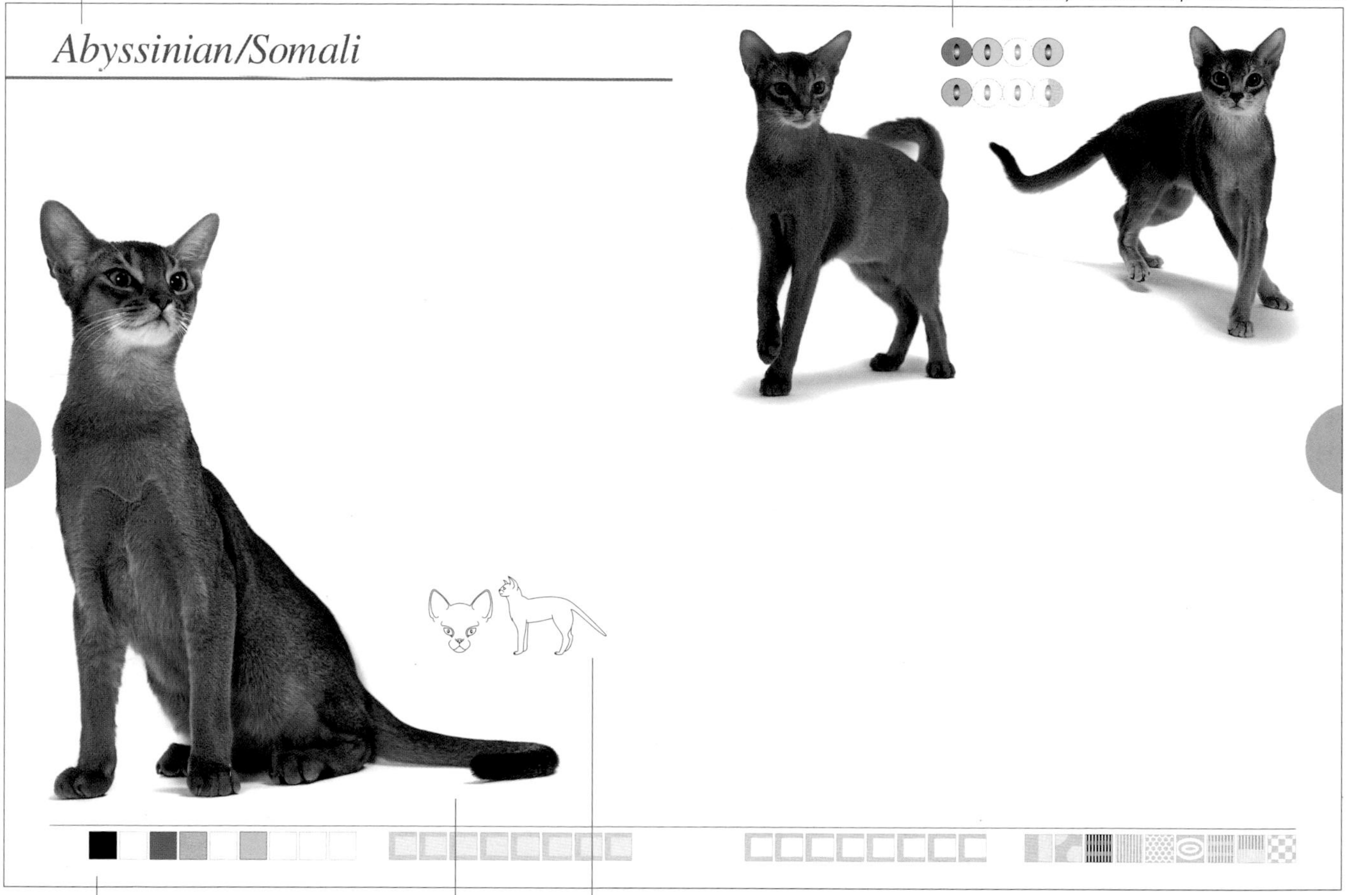

Abyssinian/Somali

Color Codes

The coat colors and patterns that are recognized for each breed are shown. From left to right, the codes are for Traditional Colors, Sepia & Mink Colors, Pointed Colors, and Patterns. The two colors in Solid within Patterns signify eumelanin color and phaeomelanin color. If particular colors and patterns of each breed are recognized, the codes are shown in colors. If not, the codes are shown in gray.

Marbled Tabby for the Bengal and Mitted for the Birman and the Snowshoe are made for them as exceptions.

Line Drawings

They show the head shape and the body type with additional information.

Cat Information

Breed name, color & pattern, sex, and age at the time of photographing are given in this order. As to the age, ∞g0.07∞h means, for example, that the cat is seven months old.

profiles
of
cats

Abyssinian/Somali

This elegant breed of cat stands on its tiptoes, showing off a shimmering coat color that appears to glow.

General Description

The shorthaired, agouti ticked Abyssinian is distinguished from other breeds by its elegance, stance, and glowing coat. The standard requires that this cat should stand on tiptoes, high on its legs—high and proud. The Abyssinian, a consummate performer, will arch its neck and take this stance when placed on a judge's table for all to admire.

History

The Abyssinian may be one of our oldest breeds of cats, but its origin remains a mystery. Ancient Egyptian paintings and sculptures depict cats that may resemble the Abyssinian of today. According to one story, soldiers returning to England from Abyssinia (now Ethiopia) in the 1800s brought cats with them from that country. However, many breeders believe that the Abyssinian cat was developed in England, since no records have been found that document the importation of cats from Abyssinia. It is, however, generally accepted that the first Abyssinian to be exhibited was at a show in England; the first Abyssinian registration, in 1896, was entered in the stud book of the National Cat Club.

The first Abyssinians to be transported to North America from England arrived in the early 1900s, but it was not until the late 1930s that several top-quality Abyssinians were exported from Britain, forming the foundation of today's American breeding programs. The first Abyssinian to be registered in the United States was born in 1933

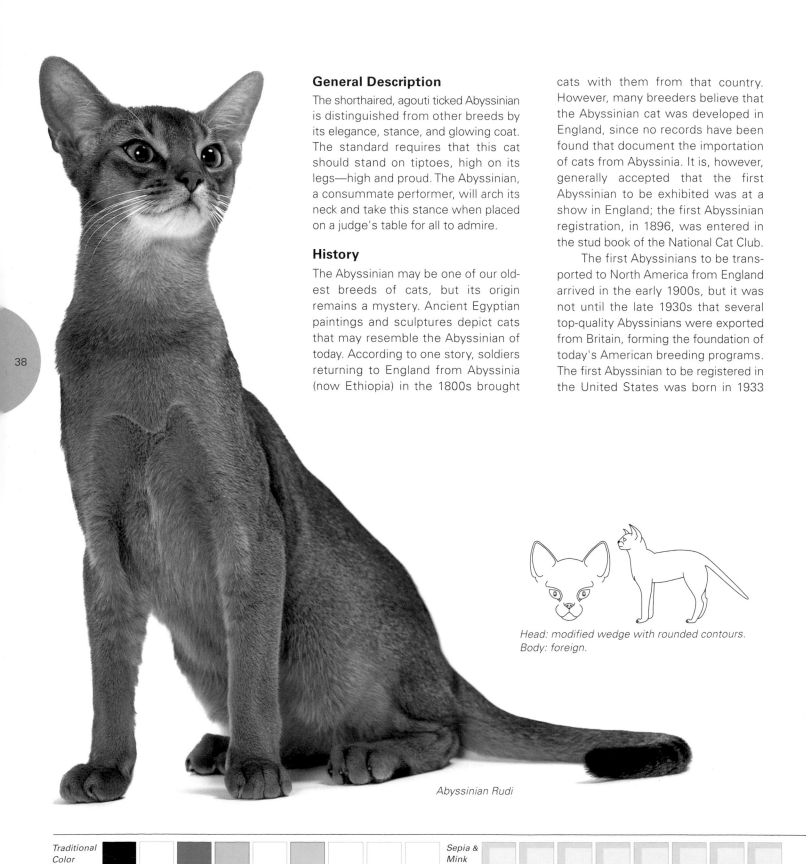

Head: modified wedge with rounded contours.
Body: foreign.

Abyssinian Rudi

Traditional Color	Rudi	Chocolate	Sorrel	Blue	Lilac	Fawn	Red	Cream	White	Sepia & Mink Color	Seal	Chocolate	Cinnamon	Blue	Lilac	Fawn	Red	Cream

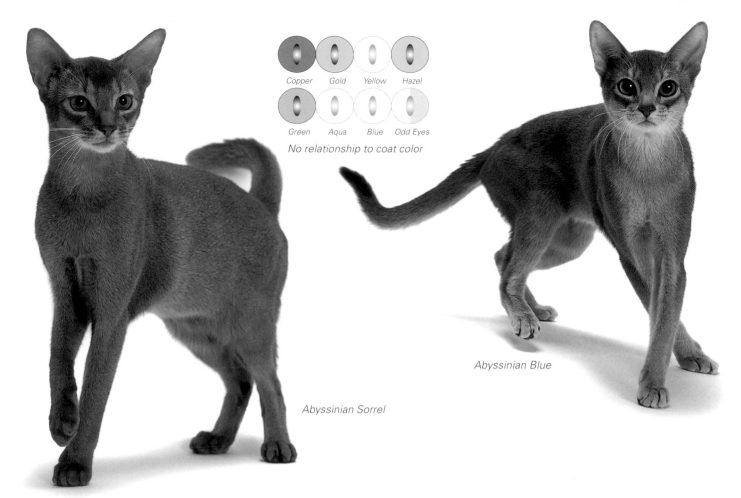

Copper · Gold · Yellow · Hazel
Green · Aqua · Blue · Odd Eyes

No relationship to coat color

Abyssinian Blue

Abyssinian Sorrel

and was paired with a male Abyssinian. The pair produced kittens whose bloodlines are present in many of today's Abyssinians. The first Abyssinian kittens in the United States were entered in Volume 19 of the Cat Fanciers' Association's (CFA) Stud Book registry around 1938.

In the United States, the general form and body structure, also called "type," of the modern Abyssinian has changed drastically from the earlier more moderate type. In the past the Abyssinian was judged on its coat and color. If the cat had a plush coat and a ruddy color, a judge could ignore the type. Today the Abyssinian, in North America, is judged on type first, color second, wih coat texture to be considered last. In other countries, however, the coat and color may still be considered more important than the type. Certain organizations may limit the accepted colors to the ruddy and the sorrel; while in others, the colors are expanded to include silver.

Appearance

The Abyssinian is a medium-sized cat, slender and lithe, strong and muscular. The body is foreign in type, with tall,

slender legs. The head has a modified wedge shape with softened, rounded contours. The ears are strikingly large and set far apart—not sitting right on top of the head, but flaring outward as a continuation of the modified wedge. The large, expressive almond-shaped eyes should be slanted toward the lower base of the ear. The head ends with a firm muzzle that is neither narrow nor wide.

Color and Pattern

Concerning all the "brown" tabby colors, a brown tabby is basically a black cat. All tabbies that are not silvered have rufousing polygenes. We call them brown tabbies because the rufousing polygenes change the color of the ticking, ground color, and the indicative color. These polygenes are present in greater or lesser amounts. A small amount will result in the "yellow" band being of a beige color; cats with this coloring are referred to as "cold" tabbies. If a greater number of these polygenes are present, the beige color changes to apricot or in a high amount to a burnt sienna. The rufousing polygenes also appear to change the torso tabby pattern color to shades of warm

brown, yet leaving the color markings on the extremities of the cat dark brown or black.

The Abyssinian is recognized in the traditional category, tabby division, in the eumelanistic colors and the agouti tabby pattern only. The agouti gene causes the hair to be ticked with alternating bands of warm apricot to a deeper burnt sienna and a band of the indicative color. With the Abyssinian, the pattern is restricted to the head and the tail. There is no tabby pattern on the torso. The tail is to be without rings and the end of the tail is tipped with the indicative or marking color. An unbroken necklace (neck area) is a "withhold all awards." Broken necklaces and leg bars are considered a penalty. The head is "pencil marked" with an "M" on the forehead. At the side of each eye is a curved darker pencil line that looks like a continuation of the upper eyelid, giving the Abyssinian's head an Egyptian or Cleopatra look. A "thumb print" marking is desirable on the back of the ear. This is a very beautifully marked cat, almost as if a beautiful woman had applied eye make-up to it.

Pointed Color — Seal · Chocolate · Cinnamon · Blue · Lilac · Fawn · Red · Cream

Pattern — Solid Color · Tortoise-shell · Agouti Tabby · Mackerel Tabby · Spotted Tabby · Classic Tabby · Silver · Tipped Color · Parti-Color

Abyssinian Rudi

The Abyssinian may "carry" the other tabby patterns, but as a result of more than eighty-five years of selective breeding, these patterns (mackerel, classic) have nearly been eliminated. Therefore, an Abyssinian bred to another Abyssinian usually produces only the Abyssinian pattern.

Ruddy:
The indicative color is black. In the agouti areas, there are alternating bands of burnt sienna and brown/black; the ground color is a burnt sienna that gives a glowing, almost gleaming appearance to the coat. The tail is tipped with black.

Blue:
The indicative color is blue. The topside is a mixture of blue and apricot ticking, while the belly is apricot or burnt sienna color. There is a distinct line of demarcation between the two colors. The tail is tipped with blue.

Sorrel:
The indicative color is cinnamon. The cinnamon color, combined with burnt sienna ground color and ticking, makes the cat look red. The tail is tipped with cinnamon. To call this cinnamon-colored cat a "red Abyssinian" is misleading, as this would indicate that the cat is under the influence of the sex-linked red gene. I have seen the sex-linked red Abyssinian in Argentina and the color looks entirely different, of course. The true red Abyssinian has an apricot or burnt sienna ground color with phaeomelanin or red as the indicative color and it is sex linked (X^p).

Fawn:
The indicative color is fawn. The color is very subtle, making it difficult to see the bands of light and dark color on each hair. The fawn has a warm, pinkish buff color, with a powdered effect. In the agouti areas, the ticking consists of alternating bands of apricot and pinkish buff colors, producing a delicate warm, soft color, something like peaches and cream.

Temperament
The Abyssinian has its own way of communicating with humans, in an open and loving manner; it loves to "talk" with people, in a euphonic voice. The Abyssinian will, without hesitation, let you know when it wants your love and attention. It almost radiates its pleasure with its soothing purrs and gentle signs of affection. A loyal, loving companion, the Abyssinian is a gentle animal that may even seem to understand the feelings of its owner.

The Abyssinian is inquisitive and loves to climb; a skilled, graceful, and agile climber, this cat is adept at moving between objects without disturbing them.

Abyssinian Silver Sorrel

Abyssinian Rudi

*Right, above: Abyssinian Sorrel;
below: Abyssinian Rudi*

Somali

The "red fox" of the cat fancy. The semi-longhaired version of the Abyssinian.

General Description

The ideal Somali is a medium-sized cat with a regal appearance. The Somali should look exactly like an Abyssinian, but sporting a glorious semi-longhaired coat. Like the Abyssinian, from which it originated, it is of foreign type. The coat of the Somali has an opalescent quality, reflecting warmth of color.

History

The Somali is a longhaired Abyssinian, which originated as an undesired product of the recessive longhair recessive gene in the Abyssinian cat.

In early years, the Somali was not held in high regard. Abyssinian breeders were appalled to find these fuzzy kittens popping up in their litters, especially after all the hard work they had put into line breeding to "fix type," working with their imported English Abyssinians. These longhaired kittens were removed from their breeding programs or otherwise "swept under the carpet". Many Abyssinian breeders even refused to admit having them.

Somali Rudi

Appearance

The Somali is a beautiful cat to behold. With its large ears and bushy tail, it resembles a little red fox. The Somali is a well-proportioned, medium-sized cat with firm muscular development and foreign type. The body is medium-long and graceful. As in the Abyssinian, the neck is arched, showing off the beautiful head. The back is slightly arched, like a cat about to spring. The legs are slim, long, and well muscled. Its elevated, regal stance gives the impression that the cat is standing on tiptoes. The Somali has an agouti coat with two to three alternating bands of rufoused color on each hair.

The head is a modified wedge with rounded contours as viewed from the front. The chin should be full (never snippy), giving a rounded appearance. The large ears should follow the lines of the modified wedge; a "thumbprint" marking is desirable on the back of the ear. The brilliant, large, almond-shaped eyes range in color from yellow to green to rich copper. The eyes are accentuated by darker lid skin, encircled by a light-colored area. Above each eye appears a short vertical darker pencil stroke in the light area. At the side of each eye appears a curved darker pencil line that looks like a continuation of the upper eyelid, thus enhancing the Cleopatra look.

The Somali has a semi-longhaired double coat of medium length, soft and silky. The coat may vary in length with shorter fur across the shoulders. The double coat may make the Somali

Somali Silver Sorrel

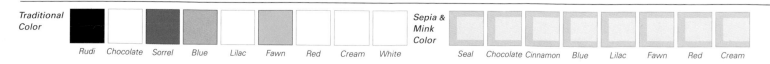

Traditional Color									Sepia & Mink Color							
Rudi	Chocolate	Sorrel	Blue	Lilac	Fawn	Red	Cream	White		Seal	Chocolate	Cinnamon	Blue	Lilac	Fawn	Red	Cream

appear to be larger and heavier than it actually is, but it also adds the wonderful fullness to the tail. The tail, indeed, resembles the tail of the Red Fox. This coat requires very little grooming and is a pleasure to hand groom by running your fingers through it.

Color and Pattern

Like the Abyssinian, the Somali is shown in the traditional category, tabby division. The colors are limited to the eumelanistic colors and the agouti tabby pattern.

Ruddy:

The indicative color is black. In the agouti areas, the hairs are ticked with two or three alternating bands of apricot or burnt sienna and dark brown. The tail is tipped with black. Longer hair will add color to an already colorful cat.

Sorrel:

The indicative color is cinnamon. In the agouti areas, the hairs are ticked with two or three alternating bands of apricot to burnt sienna and cinnamon brown. The tail is tipped with cinnamon brown.

Blue:

The indicative color is a warm, soft blue-gray. In the agouti areas, the hairs are ticked with two or three alternating bands of apricot and blue color. The undersides of the body, chest, and inside of the legs are an apricot color. The tail is tipped with a deep shade of blue.

Fawn:

The indicative color is fawn and is a warm, pinkish buff with powdered effect. In the agouti areas, it is ticked with two or three alternating bands of pale oatmeal color and a deeper shade of pinkish buff. Base hair, undersides of the body, chest, and inside of legs are a pale oatmeal color. The tail is tipped with a deep shade of pinkish buff.

Temperament

Somalis are intelligent, active cats. They talk with their owners with a soothing voice. They love to play, and like the Abyssinian, they love their owners.

Somali Fawn

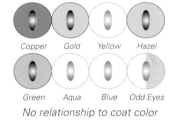

Somali Blue

43

Copper Gold Yellow Hazel

Green Aqua Blue Odd Eyes

No relationship to coat color

Head: modified wedge with rounded contours.
Body: foreign.

Somali Sorrel

Pointed Color								Pattern							
Seal	Chocolate	Cinnamon	Blue	Lilac	Fawn	Red	Cream	Solid Color	Tortoise-shell	Agouti Tabby	Mackerel Tabby	Spotted Tabby	Classic Tabby	Silver	Tipped Color	Parti-Color

American Curl/American Curl Shorthair

The American Curl is ear-resistible, with unique curling-iron ears.

Copper | Gold | Yellow | Hazel

Green | Aqua | Blue | Odd Eyes

No relationship to coat color

American Curl Blue Silver Mackerel Tabby

General Description

The first thing that is noticed is, of course, that the ears curl backwards. This gives the American Curls an almost devilish look. The American Curl may be a longhaired or a shorthaired cat. It is a rather stately cat with a semi-foreign body.

Appearance

The ideal American Curl is an intermediate cat with no extremes (except for the ears).

The head is a "modified wedge" with soft, gentle contours. In the pro-

file, the nose is straight with a slight rise to the forehead. The ears are moderately large, curving back in a smooth arc without touching the back of the ear or the head. The eyes are moderately large and walnut in shape. The body structure of the American Curl is considered semi-foreign, with medium bone structure. American Curls are elegant, graceful cats, and should never be massive or "heavy." There is little undercoat, resulting in non-matting hair that is silky and lies flat on the body. This makes the American Curl extremely easy to care for, as little

grooming is required. The long hair is not the long hair that one would associate with the Persian; it is a semi-longhair, with a tail that is full and plumed.

Color

All categories, all divisions, all colors. This means that any color or pattern that TICA recognizes is acceptable. In TICA, the American Curl is allowed to have an open registry until the year 2001, thus allowing the American Curl to incorporate the "street" knowledge of the non-pedigreed cats into its gene pool.

Traditional Color

Black | Chocolate | Cinnamon | Blue | Lilac | Fawn | Red | Cream | White

Sepia & Mink Color

Seal | Chocolate | Cinnamon | Blue | Lilac | Fawn | Red | Cream

American Curl Silver Mackerel Tabby & White

American Curl White

American Curl Brown Torbie & White

Head: broad modified wedge without flat planes.
Body: semi-foreign.

Ears

American Curls are born with straight ears. The ears do not begin to curl until the kittens are two to ten days old. The kittens enter a "transitional" phase that lasts until about 16 weeks of age. During this stage, the ears begin the change: they may uncurl or curl more tightly.

The curled ears are the result of a dominant gene. Therefore, if the sire and dam are heterozygous, the resulting litter could be all straight ears, some curled ears, or all curled ears. If an American Curl is bred to a "non-pedigreed" cat, the results could be the same. It is all in the luck of the way the genes line up.

First degree curl is a slight curl at the very tips of the ears; with this characteristic cats are considered pet quality.

Second degree curl of the ears is an arc ranging from 45 degrees to less than 90 degrees; cats with second degree curl may be considered for breeding purposes, but are not considered show quality.

Pointed Color

Seal | Chocolate | Cinnamon | Blue | Lilac | Fawn | Red | Cream

Pattern

Solid Color | Tortoise-shell | Agouti Tabby | Mackerel Tabby | Spotted Tabby | Classic Tabby | Silver | Tipped Color | Parti-Color

American Curl Red Mackerel Tabby

Third degree curl of the ears is the curliest, having a curl from 90 to 180 degrees (tips not touching the back of the ear or the head, but pointing toward the center of the base of the skull). Cats with third degree curl of the ears as well as the correct conformation would be considered show quality.

History

In June 1981 in Lakewood, California, a longhaired silky black female kitten with unusual ears wandered up to the doorstep of Joe and Grace Ruga, the founders of the breed. They named the cat Shulamith, which, according to the breeder, means "black but comely."

In December 1981, Shulamith delivered her first litter of kittens. There were four kittens; two had the same curly ears as Shulamith. This was the true beginning of the American Curl.

In September 1987, The International International Cat Association (TICA) accepted the American Curl Longhair for Championship.

American Curls are now recognized for Championship status in most cat organizations in North America.

Temperament

The American Curl is extremely intelligent, full of curiosity, and craves human companionship.

American Curls are nice, even-tempered cats, not overly talkative, but will not hesitate in letting you know when they need something or want your attention. They are laid back, and adapt with ease to almost any home situation and other animals.

American Curl Tortie Lynx Point

AMERICAN CURL SHORTHAIR

The American Curl's devilish, curled-back ears make this breed different from all others.

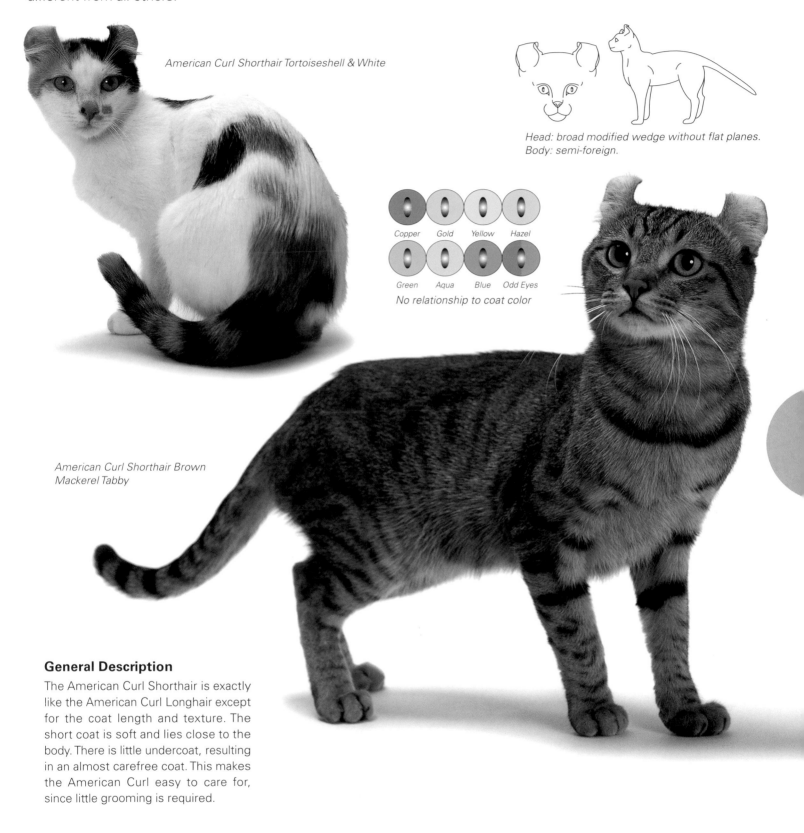

American Curl Shorthair Tortoiseshell & White

Head: broad modified wedge without flat planes.
Body: semi-foreign.

Copper · Gold · Yellow · Hazel
Green · Aqua · Blue · Odd Eyes

No relationship to coat color

American Curl Shorthair Brown
Mackerel Tabby

General Description

The American Curl Shorthair is exactly like the American Curl Longhair except for the coat length and texture. The short coat is soft and lies close to the body. There is little undercoat, resulting in an almost carefree coat. This makes the American Curl easy to care for, since little grooming is required.

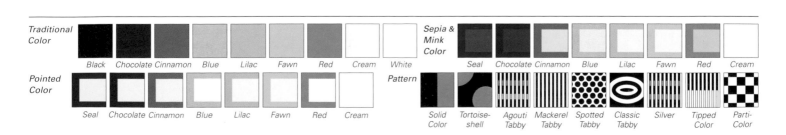

Traditional Color									Sepia & Mink Color							
Black	Chocolate	Cinnamon	Blue	Lilac	Fawn	Red	Cream	White	Seal	Chocolate	Cinnamon	Blue	Lilac	Fawn	Red	Cream

Pointed Color									Pattern								
Seal	Chocolate	Cinnamon	Blue	Lilac	Fawn	Red	Cream		Solid Color	Tortoise-shell	Agouti Tabby	Mackerel Tabby	Spotted Tabby	Classic Tabby	Silver	Tipped Color	Parti-Color

The American Shorthair is the beautiful "working" cat of the United States, the breed that should feel like handling a sack of oats.

General Description

The old standard stated that the American Shorthair should feel like a sack of oats. As I was a city person, I did not have the foggiest idea what a sack of oats felt like, until it was explained to me. There are two sacks; one is filled with hardened concrete and the other is filled with oats. The sack of concrete is heavy, but it is not pliable. The sack of oats is heavy, but pliable. This is the American Shorthair.

Appearance

The other indicative feature is the square muzzle. Can you in visualize the small box of wooden matches? Fine! Now, attach it to a cat's head, and you have the muzzle. This breed developed this muzzle for a very good reason: to catch small animals for food with its steel-trap jaws. The coat is an all-weather coat, meaning it is a hard, light reflective coat; it is not a soft, silky, or plush coat.

The ASH, as we call the breed, has a strong semi-cobby body. The head is nice and broad, with a medium-length strong, wide muzzle. The medium-sized ears are set rather wide apart, in keeping with the broad head. The standard calls for large, round eyes that are set wide apart.

May I explain a little more about the muzzle and profile? You do not want to see a "Persian" or Exotic head type: short muzzle and a nose break. There has got to be a stop or a change in direction from the brow to the beginning of the nose, but not in indentation. You do not want to see any resemblance of a "Pug" face; that look would be too extreme and not at all what an ASH should look like. The face should be "sweet", with nothing too extreme.

Color and Pattern

The American Shorthair is known for the beautiful silver classic pattern so carefully cultivated in this breed. The classic pattern is beautiful in itself; silver it and you have this wonderful contrast of black and silver.

There are other colors and patterns seen in the American, the brown and red tabbies, as well as the other tabby colors and solids.

The American Shorthair is shown in all divisions, all colors of the traditional category.

Copper	Gold	Yellow	Hazel
Green	Aqua	Blue	Odd Eyes

To conform to coat color

American Shorthair Silver Classic Tabby

Traditional Color	Black	Chocolate	Cinnamon	Blue	Lilac	Fawn	Red	Cream	White	Sepia & Mink Color	Seal	Chocolate	Cinnamon	Blue	Lilac	Fawn	Red	Cream

48

American Shorthair Silver Classic Tabby

Head: broad, rounded.
Body: semi-cobby.

American Shorthair Black

History

In the beginning, the American Shorthair was a cat of the streets, the barnyards, and the countryside. Most probably the cats originated from the British Shorthair brought to North America by European settlers to protect the cargo from mice and rats. It has been reported that records indicate that several cats arrived on the "Mayflower." Once ashore they interbred and adapted to their new outdoor environment. Remember, the early settlers settled in a very cold and harsh winter climate. In these elements, only the strong would survive.

As the United States grew in population, so did the introduction of foreign breeds during the early part of the 20th century. The Domestics (as they were known then) bred to these cats and it was not long before the "look" of the Domestic changed to being that of a mixture

American Shorthair, Brown Classic Tabby

Pointed Color								Pattern								
Seal	Chocolate	Cinnamon	Blue	Lilac	Fawn	Red	Cream	Solid Color	Tortoise-shell	Agouti Tabby	Mackerel Tabby	Spotted Tabby	Classic Tabby	Silver	Tipped Color	Parti-Color

American Shorthair Blue Classic Tabby

American Shorthair Brown Classic Torbie & White

of the Siamese or Persians. A group of dedicated breeders who wanted to preserve the earlier look of the Domestics set about doing selective breeding, in order to see the exquisite show cats we see today.

The breed has also gone through a name change. In the beginning, they were called Domestic Shorthairs. In 1966, the name was changed to American Shorthairs because the breeders felt this name reflected this wonderful "all-American cat."

Among the early breeders was the all-time famous Whitney Abt; the name of her American Shorthair cattery was Grey Horse Farm. Whitney was also the founder of CROWN, a now defunct cat registry. Among her well-known Grand Champions was a cat by the name of Perfect Gem. So the story goes, Whitney had retired Gem for several years. Later, she decided to take her out of retirement and asked the show manager to place Gem's cage in the front of the show hall entrance, so she could be seen by all exhibitors when they vetted their

cats in, and not to tell anyone that Gem was entered in the show. The exhibitors vetted their cat(s) in, saw Gem, and nearly fainted on the spot. They knew they had lost, as Gem would go Best Cat. They began to attack Whitney, almost screaming at her, saying "why did you do this?," "why didn't you leave her in retirement?" Whitney sweetly turned to them and said, "I have given you five years to catch up with me. If you have not done so, you deserve to lose."

Temperament

American Shorthairs require little

grooming and are to be considered a low-maintenance cat. They are well adapted to apartment living. They ask for nothing, make no demands on your life, and give back love in return.

The American is a very quiet, sweet cat that takes life in its stride with nothing bothering it too much. A person can walk into a household with eight or ten Americans and never know that many cats are living there, in perfect harmony with the human household. They are wonderful with children and gentle companions for the adults.

American Shorthair Silver Spotted Tabby

American Shorthair Silver Classic Tabby

AMERICAN WIREHAIR

Relatively rare, the American Wirehair is very much like the American Shorthair, except for its "steel wool" coat.

General Description

Based on my limited experience with one American Wirehair and seeing photographs of others, it would appear that the American Wirehair is not as robust as the American Shorthair. Also, it does not have the pronounced square muzzle for which the American Shorthair is noted.

The coat is the characteristic that separates the American Wirehair from all other breeds. The American Wirehair's unusual coat is the result of a spontaneous dominant mutation. All three hair types are present in this breed: guard, awn, and down, resulting in a nice dense medium-length coat.

History

The wirehair coat began as a spontaneous mutation in a litter of upstate New York farm cats in 1966. American Wirehairs have been accepted in TICA since the association's inception (1979).

Appearance

In all my years of judging, I have only seen one American Wirehair. This was Frizzie Borden, owned by Vickie Shields. Frizzie looked like an American Shorthair, except she was medium in build and, of course, had hair like "steel wool."

The head should be of medium size, in keeping with the medium-sized body. As in the American Shorthair, everything about the head is round, with gentle contours. The cheekbones, however, should be high. The eyes are round and medium in size. The ears are medium in size and set moderately

American Wirehair Black & White

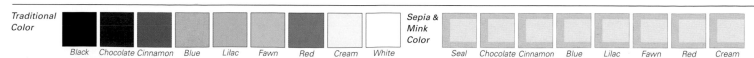

Traditional Color: Black, Chocolate, Cinnamon, Blue, Lilac, Fawn, Red, Cream, White

Sepia & Mink Color: Seal, Chocolate, Cinnamon, Blue, Lilac, Fawn, Red, Cream

American Wirehair Tortoiseshell & White
Head: round. Body: semi-cobby.

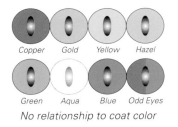

Copper   Gold   Yellow   Hazel

Green   Aqua   Blue   Odd Eyes

No relationship to coat color

apart. The medium-sized body should be a rectangular shape, rather boxy in appearance. The bone structure is medium, not as substantial as that of the American Shorthair.

Color and Pattern

American Wirehairs come in a range of Traditional Category colors, patterns, and eye colors.

Temperament

Like the American Shorthair, the American Wirehair is playful, affectionate, and loving. Owners also describe their cats as muscular and independent, agile and active. This cat rules the roost, taking no nonsense from other cats.

53

American Wirehair White

Pointed Color

Seal   Chocolate   Cinnamon   Blue   Lilac   Fawn   Red   Cream

Pattern

Solid Color   Tortoiseshell   Agouti Tabby   Mackerel Tabby   Spotted Tabby   Classic Tabby   Silver   Tipped Color   Parti-Color

Bengal

The Bengal is a beautiful, exotic-looking cat with a leopard-like color and pattern.

Bengal Brown Marbled Tabby

Bengal Brown Spotted Tabby

General Description

The Bengal does not look exactly like its ancestor, the Asian Leopard Cat. Some Bengals do have wonderful large spots or smaller rosettes, resembling the pattern of the Asian Leopard Cat. The Bengal most certainly does not have the temperament of its ancestor. In order for the Bengal to be shown in TICA, the cat must be four generations away from the Asian Leopard Cat. Bengals are loving, intelligent cats that are caring and affectionate companions to their owners. Breeders are so intent on breeding sweet-tempered Bengals that disposition is written in the Bengal's standard.

History

In the 1960s Jean Mill (Millwood Cattery) crossed a female Asian Leopard Cat (ALC) with a black domestic shorthair cat. She was told that a breeding between the two would not produce any kittens. Much to her surprise, a female kitten was born; Jean named her "Kin Kin." Once again the experts said that Kin Kin would be sterile. Jean bred Kin Kin back to her father; she did produce a litter of

kittens of which some were spotted and some were black. Jean then gave up her efforts to produce an ALC-domestic hybrid, at least temporarily.

In the early 1970s, William Engler, a zookeeper, experimented with crossing ALCs and domestics, but no Bengals are known to have come from these crosses. The name Bengal is attributed to William Engler, derived from the scientific name of the ALC, *felis bengalensis* or *prionailurus ben-*

Traditional Color									Scpia & Mink Color							
Black	Chocolate	Cinnamon	Blue	Lilac	Fawn	Red	Cream	White	Seal	Chocolate	Cinnamon	Blue	Lilac	Fawn	Red	Cream

galensis. Another early name for the breed was Leopardettes.

In the early 1980s, Jean Mill resumed her breeding program by crossing several domestics with an ALC. The resulting kittens formed the foundation of today's entire Bengal breed.

The Bengal was first recognized as a New Breed (non-championship status) by TICA in 1984. The brown spotted tabby was recognized for Championship status (TICA) in 1991; the marble pattern and the seal sepia, seal mink, and seal point in 1994.

Appearance

The Bengal is a strong, powerful, and relatively large-boned cat. Males range in weight from ten to eighteen pounds; females may be slightly smaller. The Bengal should have small, rounded ears set back on the head, intense facial markings, and large round eyes, a wide nose, and puffy whisker pads. Leopard-like spots, rosettes, or marbled patterns set them apart from the other breeds of cats.

Color and Pattern

Recognized in the tabby division, spotted tabby (spotted or rosette) and marble patterns. Brown tabby, seal sepia tabby, seal lynx point, and seal mink tabby.

The Bengal does not acquire its true adult coloration until the age of one year. The rufousing polygenes are slow to kick in. These polygenes change the ground color and banding from a drab beige to almost burnt sienna color; they also cause the extremities of the cat to be black, while the torso tabby pattern colors are shades of brown. In my opinion, the Abyssinian, Somali, and Bengal are Golden Tabbies.

The spotting pattern is unusual in that the spots align horizontally instead of vertically or in a circle (following the classic pattern). Rosettes add not only a spectacular pattern but also color variation, from light brown to a reddish brown.

Copper	Gold	Yellow	Hazel
Green	Aqua	Blue	Odd Eyes

To conform to coat color

Head: modified wedge with rounded contours.
Body: long and substantial.

Bengal Seal Mink Marbled Tabby

Pointed Color								Pattern								
Seal	Chocolate	Cinnamon	Blue	Lilac	Fawn	Red	Cream	Solid Color	Tortoise-shell	Agouti Tabby	Mackerel Tabby	Spotted Tabby	Marbled Tabby	Silver	Tipped Color	Parti-Color

Second-generation mixture of Asian Leopard Cat (one quarter Asian Leopard Cat) Brown Spotted Tabby

The Bengal is curious and entertaining. Some enjoy playing in water (make sure your fish tank is well covered) and even bathing with their owners. Many Bengals adore fresh water and can be found drinking from running faucets by "cupping" their paws for drinking.

The Bengal is extremely talkative, possessing an exceptional vocabulary of meows ranging from a low, gravelly voice to a loud (if the circumstances require) string of strong meows. The Bengal is more than willing to make known its pleasure or displeasure. A window bird feeder will cause the cat to chirp happily at the birds, which will delight in tormenting the cat (especially if the window is closed).

The marbled pattern is probably the most enchanting and colorful of the tabby patterns. It is similar to the classic, but instead of the circular pattern, try to imagine a rectangle, outlined with brown and filled with marbled shades of lighter brown, that has been skewed and stretched the length of the side of the body. The rest of the cat is covered with spots and rosettes.

All that glitters is gold! Add glitter to the coat and you have a cat that shines, it glitters, it shimmers. Is it any wonder that the Bengal is an admired, coveted breed of cat?

Seal lynx points, sometimes called snow leopards by Bengal breeders, are the result of the pointed gene, giving the cats brilliant blue eyes. Some Bengal breeders also refer to all of the pointed Bengals (seal sepias, seal lynx points, and seal minks) as snow leopards. The sepia Bengals have deep yellow or gold eye color, while the mink Bengals have aqua eye color. It is sometimes difficult to distinguish a sepia from a mink as the basic coat color, seal, is the same. One cannot always depend on the eye color to indicate the type, because the eye color may change depending on the age of the cat.

Temperament

"Temperament must be unchallenging. Any sign of definite challenge shall disqualify. Cat may exhibit fear, seek to flee, or generally complain aloud, but may not threaten to harm. Bengals should be confident, alert, curious, and friendly cats." (from the TICA Bengal Standard, 05/01/99)

Bengal Brown Marbled Tabby

Bengal Brown Spotted Tabby

Bengal Brown Spotted Tabby

56

Birman

This majestic longhaired particolor pointed cat has striking blue eyes and white laces and gloves on the feet. The Birman is known as the Sacred Cat of Burma.

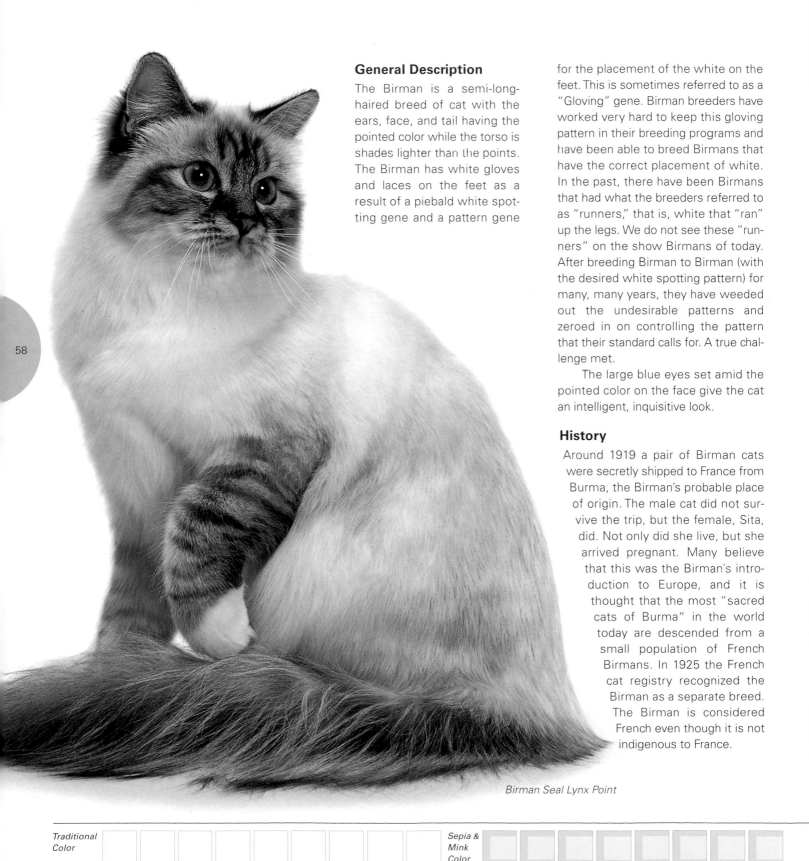

General Description

The Birman is a semi-long-haired breed of cat with the ears, face, and tail having the pointed color while the torso is shades lighter than the points. The Birman has white gloves and laces on the feet as a result of a piebald white spotting gene and a pattern gene for the placement of the white on the feet. This is sometimes referred to as a "Gloving" gene. Birman breeders have worked very hard to keep this gloving pattern in their breeding programs and have been able to breed Birmans that have the correct placement of white. In the past, there have been Birmans that had what the breeders referred to as "runners," that is, white that "ran" up the legs. We do not see these "runners" on the show Birmans of today. After breeding Birman to Birman (with the desired white spotting pattern) for many, many years, they have weeded out the undesirable patterns and zeroed in on controlling the pattern that their standard calls for. A true challenge met.

The large blue eyes set amid the pointed color on the face give the cat an intelligent, inquisitive look.

History

Around 1919 a pair of Birman cats were secretly shipped to France from Burma, the Birman's probable place of origin. The male cat did not survive the trip, but the female, Sita, did. Not only did she live, but she arrived pregnant. Many believe that this was the Birman's introduction to Europe, and it is thought that the most "sacred cats of Burma" in the world today are descended from a small population of French Birmans. In 1925 the French cat registry recognized the Birman as a separate breed. The Birman is considered French even though it is not indigenous to France.

Birman Seal Lynx Point

Traditional Color									Sepia & Mink Color							
Black	Chocolate	Cinnamon	Blue	Lilac	Fawn	Red	Cream	White		Seal	Chocolate	Cinnamon	Blue	Lilac	Fawn	Red	Cream

Head: round.
Body: medium long and substantial.

Copper Gold Yellow Hazel

Green Aqua Blue Odd Eyes

No relationship to coat color

Birman Seal Point

By the end of World War II, only two Birmans were left alive in Europe, and a program of outcrossing was necessary in order to reestablish the breed. By 1955, devotees of the Birman had established sufficient generations of Birman-to-Birman litters to qualify the sacred cat of Burma as a breed once more. The first Birmans to be exported came to the United States in 1959 and to Great Britain in 1965. The Birman was recognized in the United States by the CFA in 1967 and in TICA from its inception. This breed is now known throughout most of the world.

Legend

In the ancient temples of Burma there once lived white cats with golden eyes that were the devoted companions of Kittah priests. It was believed these cats carried the souls of their beloved priests to heaven and so were treated as honored guests in the temples. One priest, the High Lama, had dedicated his life to the service of Tsun Kyan-Kse, the goddess with sapphire-blue eyes and golden hair who supervised the transmigration of souls, allowing some to live again in a holy animal. One night, as the High Lama lay dying, his companion cat, Sinh, climbed upon him, faced the Tsun Kyan-Kse, and appealed for the transmutation of the High Lama's soul. As the High Lama took his last breath, his soul entered Sinh's body. The cat's body began to transform. His golden eyes turned sapphire blue like those of the goddess. His previously white coat took on a golden mist reflecting the goddess's hair. His ears, nose, tail, and legs turned dark like the earth, marking the impurity of all that touches the ground, yet where his paws touched the silk of his master's holy garments they turned a dazzling white, reflecting the purity of his master's soul. Seven days after keeping a loyal vigil by his

Birman Seal Point

Pointed Color

Seal Chocolate Cinnamon Blue Lilac Fawn Red Cream

Pattern

Solid Color Tortoise-shell Agouti Tabby Tabby (Lynx) Spotted Tabby Classic Tabby Silver Tipped Color Parti-Color

master, Sinh died, carrying his master's soul to heaven. Upon Sinh's death, all the other cats in the temple were also transformed, miraculously acquiring sapphire-blue eyes, pure white feet, and coats misted with gold.

Appearance

The sacred cat of Burma is imposing in appearance, muscular, and is powerfully built, medium to large in size. This is a stocky cat with hair that does not easily mat.

The medium-sized, round head is strong and broad. The forehead slopes back with a slight transverse flat spot in the middle of the forehead just above the eye ridge. There is a definite stop between the forehead and the Roman nose; the nostrils are set low. The medium-sized ears should be set moderately far apart. The almost-round blue eyes are large and should be wide set.

Color and Pattern

The Birman is shown in all colors of the pointed category, particolor division, mitted pattern only.

The front feet have white gloves ending in an even line across the paws at the third joint. The back feet have white gloves that extend straight up the back of the legs, ending in a point approximately halfway up the hock; these are referred to as "laces." Evenly matched gloves and laces are desirable. The coat has a golden cast, as if misted with gold.

Temperament

Birmans are healthy, intelligent cats. Relaxed, easygoing members of their human families, Birmans have well-balanced and tolerant personalities. Given their peaceful nature, most Birmans easily adapt to homes with children or with other cats and dogs. They give the impression of quiet power and harmony through pensive, sweet eyes. The robust, hardy breed adapts easily to rural or city life and is reported to be resistant to disease.

60

Birman Lilac Point

above: Birman Blue Point.
below: Birman Lynx Point.

Bombay

The Bombay is the sleek black panther of the cat fancy.

Bombay Black

General Description

The Bombay is a man-made breed. This is a shorthaired cat and comes only in black color. It is noted for its sleek black coat, enormous strength, and large, copper-penny-colored eyes.

History

The Bombay was developed by Nikki Horner, then of Louisville, Kentucky, in the late 1950s. She set out to create a miniature black panther by crossing a sable Burmese with a black American Shorthair. Her first attempt was disappointing, but, a few years later, when working with different cats, she began to get the results she was looking for: a cat with good muscular development and a very short, close-lying black coat. The Bombay was accepted for championship by the CFA in 1976. It was accepted in TICA from the very inception of the organization.

Appearance

This is a shorthaired, semi-cobby, medium-sized cat with substantial bone structure, good muscular development, and a surprising weight for its size. The Bombay may appear to be a medium-sized cat, but when one picks it up, it is quite heavy. It should have a strong, solid feel to it. There is nothing delicate about this cat.

The head is round, topped off with medium-sized ears that are set wide. In profile, a moderate stop, or slight indentation at the bridge of the nose, should be visible. The forehead is rounded, but not domed; the muzzle is short, but not "pugged" or "snubbed"; and the body is semi-cobby. Everything about this cat should be moderate; nothing is extreme. Please note that in some organizations, the Bombay does indeed have

Traditional Color

Black	Chocolate	Cinnamon	Blue	Lilac	Fawn	Red	Cream	White

Sepia & Mink Color

Seal	Chocolate	Cinnamon	Blue	Lilac	Fawn	Red	Cream

Bombay Black

Bombay Black

Bombay Black

| Copper | Gold | Yellow | Hazel |
| Green | Aqua | Blue | Odd Eyes |

No relationship to coat color

Head: round.
Body: semi-cobby.

63

the extreme look (break in the nose and a shorter muzzle) of the Burmese.

Color and Pattern

The Bombay is shown in solid black only.

There is something magical about the combination of the deep copper eye color and the black, shiny, slick coat. The silky, "lacquer–painted" coat is wonderfully smooth to the touch.

Temperament

Many Bombays have the Burmese "purrsonality," which means they are very relaxed, friendly, intelligent, and people oriented. Some owners describe them as "lap fungus" or "velcro" because these cats always want to be close to their people. They actively seek interaction with humans and love to play games. Many will retrieve and perform tricks. If you want a bed kitty, a Bombay may be an ideal choice, because many will sleep under the covers with their human companion. Bombays may or may not be "talkative," but they are in no way as noisy as the Siamese or Orientals. They are well adapted for house or apartment living since they are generally calm and quiet in nature.

| Pointed Color | | | | | | | | Pattern | | | | | | | | |
| Seal | Chocolate | Cinnamon | Blue | Lilac | Fawn | Red | Cream | Solid Color | Tortoise-shell | Agouti Tabby | Mackerel Tabby | Spotted Tabby | Classic Tabby | Silver | Tipped Color | Parti-Color |

British Shorthair

With its plush, thick, short coat and its semi-cobby body, the British Shorthair cat is a delight to cuddle and snuggle up to— the teddy bear of the cat fancy.

General Description

The British Shorthair, the working cat of Great Britain, has a strong body and an extremely thick coat. This cat forms the genetic basis of many breeds in the United States and in Great Britain. The Selkirk Rex, for example, has the British Shorthair as a basis for its structure.

History

The British Shorthair is one of the oldest cat breeds. In fact, it has been said that its lineage goes back to ancient times, when the Romans occupied Great Britain.

After the Roman invasion of Britain, farming was begun there, and along with it came the need to protect the grain from rodents. Working cats, so called because they worked for their food and were not kept just as pets, were brought in by the Roman legions to keep the rodent population under control. These cats lived freely in the storage sheds and farms and were relatively free of human manipulation. The cat population grew in number and thrived.

When the Romans departed, Britain became isolated from the rest of the world. No new cats were imported for hundreds of years, and Britain's cats were left to breed freely within the existing feline population. The result was a cat with a sturdy body and a thick, plush coat.

In the late 1800s cat fanciers in England recognized that their native cat was attractive and worthy of note. In 1871, the world's first cat show was held in London's Crystal Palace. British Shorthairs were entered in this show and took home many high awards. By

British Shorthair Blue

Head: round.
Body: semi-cobby.

Copper   Gold   Yellow   Hazel

Green   Aqua   Blue   Odd Eyes

To conform to coat color

Traditional Color

Black   Chocolate   Cinnamon   Blue   Lilac   Fawn   Red   Cream   White

Sepia & Mink Color

Seal   Chocolate   Cinnamon   Blue   Lilac   Fawn   Red   Cream

British Shorthair Cream Spotted Tabby

British Shorthair Blue

British Shorthair Tortie & White

1889, the British Shorthair was granted recognition as a distinct breed, but by the end of the century, it fell out of favor and had to yield to the more fashionable Persian and Siamese.

During World War II, the breeding of British Shorthair cats almost came to an end as a result of food shortage. Like so many breeds, this cat nearly became extinct. Breeders were forced to cross the British Shorthair with another breed of cat just to keep the bloodlines going. They turned to the Persian, since it was the closest in type (the early Persian bore little resemblance to the modern Persian). This outcrossing resulted in the appearance of other colors and patterns besides the traditional blue.

Appearance

Strong, muscular, and powerful, the British Shorthair is a sturdy, medium to large cat with a semi-cobby torso. The head is broad and round, with a firm chin and a round, well-developed muzzle. The nose is short but never snubbed or foreshortened like that of a Persian or Exotic Shorthair. The full, chubby cheeks give the cat a

Pointed Color								Pattern								
Seal	Chocolate	Cinnamon	Blue	Lilac	Fawn	Red	Cream	Solid Color	Tortoise-shell	Agouti Tabby	Mackerel Tabby	Spotted Tabby	Classic Tabby	Silver	Tipped Color	Parti-Color

British Shorthair White

chipmunk-like appearance. If the head is properly proportioned, one should be able to "cup" the skull and muzzle with two hands. The eyes should be large, round, and expressive.

Like the Norwegian Forest Cat and the Siberian, the British Shorthair adapted to the cold weather of England by developing a very thick, short coat. The blue British Shorthair's fur feels like a plush rug and should cause the hands to tingle when stroking the cat. This breed of cat is easy to groom, since the fur does not tangle.

Color and Pattern

The British Shorthair is shown in all colors and all divisions of the traditional category.

The original British Shorthair was called "British Blue" because that was the only color the cat was shown in. Indeed, even though this cat comes in many different colors and patterns, some organizations still recognize blue as the only accepted color. The blue British have a thicker coat than that of, say, a black or a white.

Temperament

The British Shorthair is independent yet affectionate, relaxed yet curious. The male, in particular, is especially friendly to people, even to the point of being mushy. This is an extremely quiet, no-nonsense, unflappable breed of cat. British Shorthairs are well suited for apartment life, provided the apartment is not kept too warm.

66

British Shorthair Blue & White

British Shorthair Shaded Golden

British Shorthair Blue

Burmese

The Burmese is the golden-eyed brown beauty of the cat fancy.

General Description

The body type of the Burmese varies from country to country. In some countries, the Burmese has a longer body and legs, making it entirely different from those in the United States. For example, the Burmese is described in the Australian standard as a cat of foreign type; in the North American standard, it is a round, cobby, small but heavy cat.

History

The Burmese dates back to the early 1930s, when Dr. Joseph C. Thompson of San Francisco brought back a chocolate-colored cat from Burma named Wong Mau. Wong Mau was bred to a Siamese, since no other cats of her color were available for breeding. I have a picture of Wong Mau and her babies that clearly shows some pointed (cs) kittens. If Wong Mau had been a Burmese, then breeding her to a Siamese would have produced all Tonkinese (mink-colored) kittens. Wong Mau may be regarded as the first Tonkinese (although her type was certainly different from the present-day Tonkinese).

After several generations, kittens were produced with three distinct colors. This was done by breeding mink to mink. Some looked like Siamese, some looked like Wong, and some appeared to be of a solid, dark brown color (a sable Burmese will appear to be solid, but if you look closely, the points can be seen). The Burmese breed originated from these dark brown kittens.

Until the 1960s the Burmese in North America were more foreign in type. That is, the head was not the rounded shape that we see today; the body and legs were longer. The 1960s brought about changes to the Burmese type to make the head rounded and the muzzle short, there was a break in the nose, and the body became compact. We refer to this type of Burmese as the Contemporary Burmese.

A famous breeder of Burmese during the 1960s was Gladys de Fleron (Fleur de Lis cattery) of New Orleans, Louisiana. She too had shown foreign-type Burmese, until a quite different-

Burmese Sable

Traditional Color									Sepia & Mink Color							
Black	Chocolate	Cinnamon	Blue	Lilac	Fawn	Red	Cream	White	Seal	Chocolate	Cinnamon	Blue	Lilac	Fawn	Red	Cream

Copper Gold Yellow Hazel

Green Aqua Blue Odd Eyes

No relationship to coat color

69

Burmese Sable

Head: round.
Body: cobby.

Burmese Blue Sepia

looking kitten showed up in her cattery. This cat was shorter and more compact in the body than her other cats. She liked his looks and decided to keep him for herself. She named him Theebaw. Gladys showed him as an adult and took the cat fancy by storm. Theebaw proceeded to win and win and win at the shows and went on to be ACFA Cat of the Year in the 1960s. He helped to change the North American standards for Burmese, from the semi-foreign type of years past to the cobby type of today.

There were other famous Burmese that left their mark on the contemporary Burmese of today: Prince Pogo of Regal (born in 1958); Mizpah's Clancy (born in 1959); Mizpah's Fernand of Briarwood; Hill House Daniella of Shawnee; Burma Road's Detour of Senshu; Phi Line Uncas of Day-Ho (son of "Troubador" and grandson of Detour and Casey Jones); GC Good Fortune Fortunatas; GC Morningside Attsi (a Chirn Sa-Hai descendent)—just to name a few. You would also find cats of Chirn Sa-Hai cattery, owned by Beth O'Donovan (Florida, USA), in the pedigrees of many of these famous Burmese. The 1960s were indeed the turning point for the Burmese in the United States.

Appearance

The word for the Burmese is "round." Everything about this breed is round. The head, the eyes, the short muzzle, and even the chest are round.

This is a cobby breed of cat. The body is short; it should never be long or rangy. This is a rather small breed of cat (but just wait until you pick one up—they are surprisingly heavy). A male may be quite large, powerful, and strong. The females may be daintier than the males. A "barrel" chest may be seen on both sexes, but most

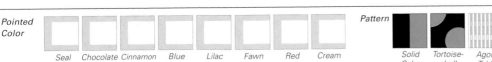

Pointed Color Seal Chocolate Cinnamon Blue Lilac Fawn Red Cream

Pattern Solid Color Tortoise-shell Agouti Tabby Mackerel Tabby Spotted Tabby Classic Tabby Silver Tipped Color Parti-Color

certainly on the full-grown male. The head should be rounded without flat planes. There should be considerable breadth between the round, yellow-to-gold eyes. In profile there should be a visible break in the line of the nose. The medium-sized ears are set well apart. Little grooming is required, since the Burmese is a "self-cleaning" cat. For show purposes, a gentle rubdown with a damp cloth or glove is all that is necessary.

Color and Pattern

The Burmese may be shown in sepia category, solid and tortoiseshell divisions.

The solid colors: sable (seal sepia), chocolate sepia, cinnamon sepia, blue sepia, lilac sepia, fawn sepia, red sepia, and cream sepia. The tortoiseshell colors are: sable tortie (seal sepia), chocolate sepia tortie, cinnamon sepia tortie, blue sepia tortie, lilac sepia tortie, and fawn sepia tortie.

The color of the Burmese is the result of a genetic mutation at the full color locus.

The Burmese is pointed; however, in the sable, these points may not be easily seen except in full sunlight. The sable (seal sepia) Burmese has dark brown points and dark brown body color, giving it the appearance of one solid color. The eye color is gold to yellow. Seal sepia and sable are color names for the same color—seal brown. TICA allowed the Burmese and the Singapura to retain the designer name *sable*. The red sepia Burmese, bred in England for many years, displays a beautiful tangerine color. In some countries, silver has recently been added to the gene pool. Is it possible to have a sepia smoke Burmese? You bet it is. The gene for the sepia color and the Inhibitor gene do not share the same locus.

Temperament

The Burmese is a happy-go-lucky, taking-everything-in-stride cat. This cat loves to be around people and demands love, but it also returns the favor by giving love, affection, and good company. Vocal and talkative, with a rather loud voice, a Burmese cat will let you know what it wants, in no uncertain terms.

Burmese Sable

Burmese Chocolate Sepia

Burmese Sable

Chartreux

The Chartreux, a natural French breed of great antiquity, is known as the Smiling Blue Cat of France.

General Description

The Chartreux is France's native working cat. This is the one breed that is delightfully out of proportion. If you're wondering what I mean, my favorite description of the Chartreux might give you a hint—a potato on toothpicks.

History

This native breed of France was noted in documents as early as the sixteenth century. It has been reported that the Chartreux descended from the "Cat of Syria," from a sixteenth-century description of a stocky cat with a woolly ash-gray coat and copper eyes. It has been further reported that the Chartreux was brought to Europe during the Crusade era. History has it that the cat's pelt was so highly prized by furriers that many of these cats were killed for their coats. The early Chartreux cats did not have an easy life; if they were not used as ratters (thus exposed to the elements), they were used for their pelts and even killed for their meat.

As with many breeds of cats, legends regarding the Chartreux's history abound. One of the most popular legends has it that the breed was named for the Carthusian monks of France, who developed Chartreuse liqueur. A recent study shows another possibility for the breed name: due to the woolly nature of their fur, the breed may have been given the name of a Spanish wool of the early eighteenth century.

During World Wars I and II the numbers of Chartreux cats dwindled. As with other endangered breeds, breeders had to take an active interest in preserving the breed. After World War I, a group of French cat breeders went to work in an effort to preserve this ancient breed by selecting only those cats that would best fit the original type of the breed. Their work was successful: in 1928, the Chartreux began to be exhibited in European cat shows. A few years later, World War II hit, and when the dust settled, there were no known natural colonies of blue cats left in France.

It was not until the 1970s that the Chartreux was introduced to the United States. It should be noted that the present-day Chartreux cat is almost identical in type and coat to its original ancestor. Unlike the standards of other breeds such as the Persian and the Siamese, the Chartreux standard has not changed over the years.

The Chartreux, still relatively rare, is now truly a breeders' cat. This cat is dearly loved and prized in France, as well as around the rest of the world.

Appearance

The Chartreux's head is broad and round; stuck on the top of the head are small to medium-sized ears that are set close together, rather than on the corners of the head. The strong jaws give the cat a smiling look. The copper eyes are large and round. The body is semi-cobby and quite substantial—like a nice, round potato. The legs are slim—hence, a potato on toothpicks!

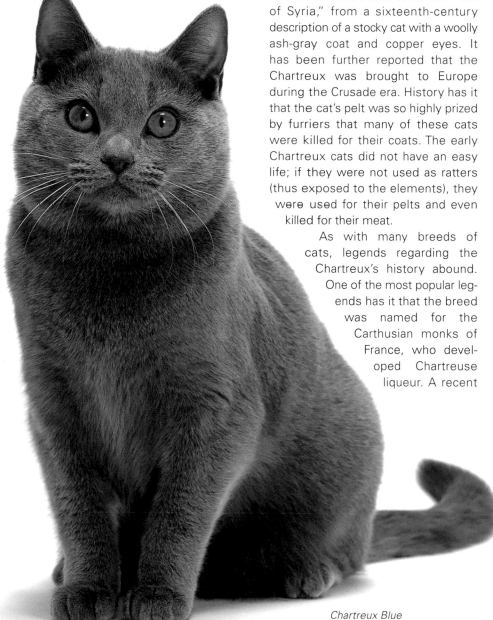

Chartreux Blue

Traditional Color									Sepia & Mink Color							
Black	Chocolate	Cinnamon	Blue	Lilac	Fawn	Red	Cream	White		Seal	Chocolate	Cinnamon	Blue	Lilac	Fawn	Red	Cream

Copper Gold Yellow Hazel

Green Aqua Blue Odd Eyes

No relationship to coat color

Chartreux Blue

Head: round.
Body: semi-cobby, medium long, sturdy with slim legs.

Chartreux Blue

The blue coat should be short and thick, never close-lying or slick. This woolly, double soft, sensuous coat adds bulk to the already robust torso. Brushing the Chartreux's coat is not advised, except during the cat's shedding period. The only grooming the Chartreux needs is some gentle stroking with your hand, but some enjoy a soft rubdown with a chamois. When being bathed, this thick coat can be just like the water-repellent, dense coat of the Norwegian Forest Cat or the Siberian—it will take several tries to get the soap and water down to the skin.

Color and Pattern

The Chartreux may be shown in the traditional category, solid division. Any shade of blue is acceptable for the coat, although a silver sheen is desirable.

Eye color is gold or copper; copper is preferred.

Temperament

One would expect a cat of this breed to have a full, strong voice, but in fact it has a tiny, wee voice. Indeed, some of the Chartreux are completely mute; they purr but are unable to meow. They are wonderful companion cats as they are quiet, calm, and reserved. They are independent and adapt quite nicely to apartment living or country living.

These cats are bulky and quite heavy, yet they adore climbing to the top of a cat tree or other high object and flying through the air to the next high object. This behavior is not associated with most of the heavier cats. Not surprisingly, these cats need plenty of room in order to do their acrobatics.

This is an extremely intelligent breed: the Chartreux will come when called by its name, it loves to run and fetch, and it much prefers your bed to its own. The Chartreux is said to have dog-like devotion to its owners (and, like a dog, it loves a good car ride) and is tolerant and gentle with small children. This cat does not look for trouble and will walk away from any aggressive or threatening situations.

Pointed Color

Seal Chocolate Cinnamon Blue Lilac Fawn Red Cream

Pattern

Solid Color Tortoise-shell Agouti Tabby Mackerel Tabby Spotted Tabby Classic Tabby Silver Tipped Color Parti-Color

Chartreux Blue

Chartreux Blue

Chartreux Blue

Chartreux Blue

Cornish Rex

The greyhound of the cat fancy, the Cornish Rex is known for its marcelled hair, egg-shaped head, and huge upright ears.

General Description

The Cornish Rex is like no other breed of cat. Everything is curly about this cat—its coat, the hair on its tail, even the whiskers. The coat is wavy and deeply, tightly marcelled—it ripples.

History

The Cornish Rex dates from 1950, when the Ennismores farmed land in Bodmin Moor, in Cornwall, England. Where there is a farm, there are sure to be cats. On this farm, a cat by the name of Serena, a tortie and white shorthair, had a litter of kittens that included a male (later named Kallibunker) with a very unusual coat—it was in waves. Even stranger, his type was different from that of his mother; his head and body were long. Kallibunker was bred back to his mother; this breeding produced more wavy-coated kittens. These were later to be called Rex, after the rabbits of the same name. All Cornish Rex cats trace their ancestry back to Kallibunker.

In 1957, a pregnant Cornish Rex was exported to a breeder in California. The litter consisted of two rex kittens. One was sent to Fan-T-Cee cattery; the other was sent to Daz-Zling cattery. These kittens were to be the foundation of all the Cornish Rex in America—Lil of Fan-T-Cee and Marmaduke of Daz-Zling.

Helen Weiss (Daz-Zling) bred Marmaduke to her Siamese cats, giving the breed the finer bones of the Siamese, and a longer head, body, and tail. This outcrossing also introduced the pointed gene into the gene pool.

Cornish Rex Tortoiseshell & White

| Copper | Gold | Yellow | Hazel |
| Green | Aqua | Blue | Odd Eyes |

No relationship to coat color

| Traditional Color | Black | Chocolate | Cinnamon | Blue | Lilac | Fawn | Red | Cream | White | Sepia & Mink Color | Seal | Chocolate | Cinnamon | Blue | Lilac | Fawn | Red | Cream |

Head: egg-shaped.
Body: Oriental with tuck-up.

left: Cornish Rex Tortoiseshell.
right: Cornish Rex Red Mackerel Tabby & White

Cornish Rex Blue Point & White

Pointed Color							
Seal	Chocolate	Cinnamon	Blue	Lilac	Fawn	Red	Cream

Pattern								
Solid Color	Tortoise-shell	Agouti Tabby	Mackerel Tabby	Spotted Tabby	Classic Tabby	Silver	Tipped Color	Parti-Color

Cornish Rex Blue

Cornish Rex Black Smoke & White

Appearance

The chic-looking Cornish Rex is called the greyhound of the cat world because the backbone follows an upward curve that causes the stomach to be "drawn up," forming a "tuck up" like that of a greyhound. Therefore, the Cornish Rex is referred to as the greyhound of the Cat Fancy.

This cat should be medium in size, long, and slim. If it were not for the curly coat, I would say that this breed is sleek-looking. This is the only breed that has an egg-shaped head. Even the top of the head is rounded instead of flat. The close-set ears are huge and set high on the head. The medium-sized oval eyes are set just an eye's width apart.

In some organizations, great emphasis is placed on the waviness of the coat, thus allowing for more leeway in the type. Indeed, I have judged Cornish Rex in some countries where the only thing the cats had in common was the wavy coat. TICA requires that the cat have the type mentioned above plus the wavy coat. The wavy coat is not a permanent fixture, since (depending on the time of year) the Cornish Rex may lose some of the wavy coat or indeed some of its fur. Also, if a female has been in season for a long time, her hormones may influence the wave of her coat. Many breeders feel that a rex coat of the Cornish Rex, Devon Rex, Selkirk Rex, and La Perm is directly under the influence of hormones.

Color and Pattern

The Cornish Rex is recognized in all colors of all divisions.

Due to the curly coat, the colors ripple, making the cat almost appear to shimmer.

Temperament

An attractive addition to any household, this charming and talkative designer feline makes an excellent, though extremely active, pet. The clown-like Cornish Rex cat's playful personality and boundless curiosity drives it to investigate everything. Its affectionate nature makes it a very sweet and loving companion that craves attention.

Cornish Rex Black Smoke & White

Cornish Rex Black Smoke & White

Devon Rex

The Devon Rex is the pixie of the cat world, sporting huge, bat-like ears and wavy hair.

General Description

One can describe the individual parts of the Devon Rex, but it is difficult to describe the complete cat. One can say it has a modified wedge with rounded contours, that it has a semi-foreign type, that it is a shorthaired cat with wavy hair, but the parts cannot be described quite so simply. It is almost as if each part of the Devon Rex is different and yet put together to form this strangely wonderful-looking cat.

History

In 1950 a new curly-coat mutation was discovered in the domestic feline. These cats were born in Cornwall, England; they would be the foundation of the Cornish Rex.

The Devon Rex appeared in 1960 in Devon, England. At first breeders tried to breed the Devon Rex to the Cornish Rex, in hope of producing rex-coated kittens. This did not happen. The resulting kittens had straight hair and presented no improvement in type. Breeders introduced other breeds into the gene pool, but these early outcrosses did not produce the desired type. Outcrossing was then done only when necessary for the health and coat density of the breed. The Devon Rex gene produces Devon Rex type; in second-generation kittens, plain-coated kittens are of domestic type, but the curlies all have Devon type.

Devon Rex cats were first imported into the United States in 1968. This cat now enjoys championship status in most cat registering bodies throughout the world.

Appearance

The Devon Rex is a distinct breed, different from all others, with its spacious large eyes, short muzzle, prominent cheekbones, and huge, low-set ears. It is the ears that create the characteristic elf-like look. This shorthaired breed is described as medium boned. I put it in the semi-foreign type on the chart because it did not fit into the semi-cobby, but the standard does not state semi-foreign. Remember that I said this is one breed in which the parts were assembled; it may not fit into any category of body type. A stop or an indentation from the eye ridge to the beginning of the nose is necessary, providing a muzzle break and giving

Devon Rex Cinnamon Tortie Point

Copper Gold Yellow Hazel

Green Aqua Blue Odd Eyes

To conform to coat color

Traditional Color									Sepia & Mink Color							
Black	Chocolate	Cinnamon	Blue	Lilac	Fawn	Red	Cream	White	Seal	Chocolate	Cinnamon	Blue	Lilac	Fawn	Red	Cream

Devon Rex Chocolate Torbie & White

Devon Rex Chocolate & White

Devon Rex Black Smoke

the breed a head type like no other. The ears should be huge and low set. The eyes are round, large, and set rather wide apart, just above the high cheekbones. The muzzle is short, yet pronounced. The coat, produced by a genetic mutation, is soft with loose

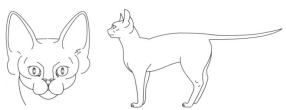

Head: modified wedge.
Body: semi-foreign.

Pointed Color							
Seal	Chocolate	Cinnamon	Blue	Lilac	Fawn	Red	Cream

Pattern								
Solid Color	Tortoise-shell	Agouti Tabby	Mackerel Tabby	Spotted Tabby	Classic Tabby	Silver	Tipped Color	Parti-Color

Devon Rex White

Devon Rex Brown Mackerel Tabby & White

waves, like the gentle waves of a rippling brook.

Color and Pattern

The Devon Rex is recognized in all colors of all divisions.

The colors of the tabby and tortie patterns may be less intense than in other breeds, due to the shortness and wavy hairs. If the ends of the hair are fragile, the tips may break off; therefore not as much pigment is present as in cats with longer hairs. However, many Devon Rex cats do have a full coat of loose wavy hairs. A lightening of the hair around the base of the ears may indicate that a cat is a smoke. At certain times, the Devon Rex may have a sparse coat due to hormonal changes, especially in kittens and young adults.

Temperament

Easygoing and delightful to be with, Devon Rex cats have a wonderful personality and truly enjoy being around people. They delight in following people around, will entertain by fetching, and will show pleasure by purring very loudly. Most Devon Rex love shiny things. They will take coins, jewelry, anything shiny and play with it. When they are tired of playing, they will take the object and hide it. A breeder told me of the time she and her husband started missing a few things, earring rings, key chains. She found the cat's "toys" one day as she was cleaning out the cabinet under the bathroom sink . . . hidden in the back corner.

A computer store in Rogue River, Oregon (where I live), had a resident white Devon Rex. The cat took great delight in greeting each customer, sitting very alert right in front of the door. Surprised customers would comment, "What in the world is that? It looks like a cat, but I have never seen a cat like that." The cat was completely at home and in full command of the shop.

83

Devon Rex Blue Mink

Devon Rex Brown Mackerel Torbie & White

Egyptian Mau

The gooseberry green-eyed Egyptian Mau is the only natural spotted domestic cat, possibly descended from a small African wildcat. *Mau* is the Egyptian word for cat.

General Description

This beautiful shorthaired breed is shy and elusive—a true living artifact.

History

The Egyptian Mau, which bears a striking similarity to cats depicted in ancient Egyptian art, dates back to 1500 B.C. and may be descended from the African wildcat *felis lyica ocreata*. The Egyptian Mau's ancestor may have been the breed of cat that was loved and worshiped by the ancient Egyptians. The Egyptian cat goddess Bast was worshiped by a cult in the city of Bubast, in the Delta region, which is now believed to be the site of the domestication of the wildcat. This area had a high concentration of snakes, and the Egyptians put the cat's hunting skills to use in order to reduce the population of snakes and other pests in the granaries.

In 1953, an Egyptian Mau owned by the Egyptian ambassador to Italy caught the eye of Princess Natalie Troubetskoy, who persuaded the ambassador to help her obtain a kitten from Cairo. He agreed, and in 1955 Egyptian Mau cats were exhibited at the Rome Cat Show and attracted the attention of British cat fanciers, who later attempted but failed to produce Egyptian Maus in Britain. The princess traveled to the United States with her three Egyptian Maus in 1956. The Egyptian Maus in

left: Egyptian Mau Bronze.
right: Egyptian Mau Silver

Egyptian Mau Black Smoke

Traditional Color									Sepia & Mink Color							
Black	Chocolate	Cinnamon	Blue	Lilac	Fawn	Red	Cream	White	Seal	Chocolate	Cinnamon	Blue	Lilac	Fawn	Red	Cream

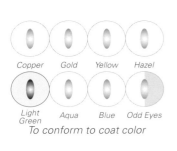

Copper Gold Yellow Hazel

Light Green Aqua Blue Odd Eyes

To conform to coat color

Egyptian Mau Silver

the United States are reportedly descended from the princess's cats.

Appearance

The Egyptian Mau should be of semi-foreign type, well muscled and medium in size. The presence of the primordial flap (skin hanging from the belly in front of the hind legs) attests to the antiquity of the breed. This flap allows the hind legs to stretch out a considerable distance, making the cat a very swift runner. The ears are medium-large in size and set well back on the head. The eyes are a rounded almond shape. The head is a modified wedge with gentle rounded contours. The Egyptian Mau has a characteristic "M" pattern on the forehead. Before the Egyptian Mau was brought to the United States, these cats usually had a scarab shape on the forehead, but this trait does not appear on most North American Egyptian Maus.

Color and Pattern

The Egyptian Mau is shown in three spotted color patterns in the traditional category and is accepted in two divisions: tabby and silver/smoke divisions.

The tabby division colors are bronze (brown spotted).

The silver/smoke division colors are silver (black silver spotted) and smoke tabby (black smoke tabby).

This black smoke tabby is not a true tabby, but a smoke with ghost-tabby markings. Ghost-tabby markings may be seen in young cats of a solid or smoke color; however, they usually disappear when the cat is an adult. The Egyptian Mau breeders have bred to retain these ghost-tabby markings in the adult cat. If the cat were a true tabby, ticked hairs would appear with the tabby pattern. The smoke Egyptian Mau does not have ticked hairs. Because the smoke Egyptian Mau has tabby markings, it has remained in the tabby division and tradition has allowed it to remain there. The beauty of the color and pattern is stunning; it resembles a moiré pattern of watered silk. The spots of the "Smoke" are very evident in direct sunlight but tend to blend into the undercoat in dimmer lighting.

Temperament

This breed of cat is extremely intelligent, moderately active, outgoing, and adventurous. The Egyptian Mau, with its affectionate personality and striking appearance, makes an exceptional companion. This breed is definitely a one-family cat, since it tends to shy away from unfamiliar people.

Head: broad modified wedge without flat planes.
Body: semi-foreign.

Egyptian Mau Bronze

Pointed Color								Pattern							
Seal	Chocolate	Cinnamon	Blue	Lilac	Fawn	Red	Cream	Solid Color	Tortoise-shell	Agouti Tabby	Mackerel Tabby	Spotted Tabby	Classic Tabby	Silver	Tipped Color	Parti-Color

Havana

The regal Havana is a chocolate- or lilac-colored shorthaired cat with intense green eyes.

General Description

The Havana is different from the Oriental Shorthair due to the puffy muzzle and the deep stop in the profile (in the area between the eyebrow and the beginning of the nose).

History

Some cat fanciers believe that these reddish brown cats originated in Siam (now Thailand), where they were kept to protect their owners from evil. Brown cats were brought to Britain, along with the Siamese, in the nineteenth century.

In 1894, certain cats entered in a London cat show were different in color (chestnut) from the pointed Siamese, but they had full color development in the coat over a Siamese body, with green instead of blue eyes. These cats were given the name Swiss Mountain Cats. This breed, however, was ignored and abandoned by the Siamese Cat Club in Britain. In the 1920s, this club made the policy statement, "The club much regrets it is unable to encourage the breeding of any but blue-eyed Siamese."

Breeders in Britain started trying to produce this lovely color of chocolate by breeding a seal point (carrying chocolate) or a chocolate point Siamese to a black cat (carrying chocolate), producing a solid chocolate kitten. More experimental breedings were done introducing the Russian Blues into the gene pool and, in this way, the dilution gene was brought in.

Havana Chocolate

Traditional Color									Sepia & Mink Color							
Black	Chocolate	Cinnamon	Blue	Lilac	Fawn	Red	Cream	White		Seal	Chocolate	Cinnamon	Blue	Lilac	Fawn	Red	Cream

Head: modified wedge with rounded contours.
Body: semi-foreign.

Copper　Gold　Yellow　Hazel

Light Green　Aqua　Blue　Odd Eyes

To conform to coat color

Havana Chocolate

Havana Chocolate

The breed was given the name Havana, probably after the Havana cigars of similar color.

Appearance

This is a striking cat of reddish brown (the breeders also refer to this color as mahogany) color and large piercing, oval green eyes. The head is different from that of other cats in that the profile shows a "ski" slope, a pronounced stop between the eyebrow and the beginning of the nose. The deep nose stop and the puffy wide muzzle are peculiar to this breed.

The cat has a good muzzle break that, when combined with the stop, allows for a muzzle with puffy whisker pads. The eyes are set low on the head, which creates the appearance of a cat looking down its nose. The forehead is high. The head is topped by large, round-tipped, alert ears that are tilted slightly forward. The combination of reddish-brown coat, green eyes, prominent round muzzle and ski-slope nose does indeed make this short-haired cat a beauty to behold.

Color and Pattern

The Havana is recognized in the solid chocolate and lilac colors in the traditional category.

The chocolate color is a rich reddish brown, not dull. Lilac, rather a difficult color to work with, is a pale tan with a touch of pink. It is not unusual for Lilacs and pointed kittens to appear in a litter of chocolate Havana bred to another chocolate Havana. Ghost tabby markings are allowed in kittens. These tabby markings should vanish when the cat is an adult. It should be noted that in countries other than the United States, Havana is considered a color, not a breed.

Temperament

Some of the early Havanas were associated with a not-too-pleasant disposition, but this may be due to the Havana's aversion to being caged or ignored. In fact, the Havana has a charming, warm disposition. Everything about the Havana is soft and gentle. These cats crave and must have attention; to be ignored by its human owner is almost more than a Havana can take. Although not a demanding cat, a Havana will softly let you know when it wants or needs you.

Havana Chocolate

Pointed Color									Pattern								
Seal	Chocolate	Cinnamon	Blue	Lilac	Fawn	Red	Cream		Solid Color	Tortoise-shell	Agouti Tabby	Mackerel Tabby	Spotted Tabby	Classic Tabby	Silver	Tipped Color	Parti-Color

Japanese Bobtail/Japanese Bobtail

A stately cat, the Japanese Bobtail has a unique short pom-pom tail and a sculptured head.

General Description

The Japanese Bobtail, a natural breed from Japan, is a long, lean, elegant cat with a pom-pom for a tail. Known for its clear, "painted-on" good luck *mi-ke* (pronounced mee-kay) pattern, the Japanese Bobtail comes in short- and longhaired varieties. The eyes are set into the skull, with a pronounced slant when viewed in profile.

History

It appears that the first domestic cats arrived in Japan from China or Korea at least one thousand years ago. The Japanese Bobtail has existed in Japan for many centuries and may be seen on ancient Japanese scrolls and paintings. Two lovely longhaired Japanese Bobtails are depicted in a large fifteenth-century painting that hangs in the Freer Gallery of Art in the Smithsonian Institution in Washington, D.C. The Japanese Bobtail was first brought to the United States in 1968, attracting the interest of American cat fanciers.

left: Japanese Bobtail Blue & White.
right: Japanese Bobtail Black & White

Appearance

The Japanese Bobtail should present the overall impression of a medium-sized cat with long, clean lines and medium bone structure. The large, oval eyes, combined with high cheekbones and a long parallel nose, lends a distinctive Japanese cast to the face, especially in the profile, which is quite different from that of the other breeds. The standard calls for a long nose that is well defined by two parallel lines from the tip to the brow; there is a gentle dip at or just below the eye level. The muzzle should be fairly broad, rounding into a whisker break. The eyeball shows a shallow curvature and should not bulge beyond the cheekbone or forehead.

Its short tail should resemble a rabbit's tail, with the hair fanning out like a pom-pom. This pom-pom effec-

Japanese Bobtail Black & White

Traditional Color	Black	Chocolate	Cinnamon	Blue	Lilac	Fawn	Red	Cream	White	Sepia & Mink Color	Seal	Chocolate	Cinnamon	Blue	Lilac	Fawn	Red	Cream

Longhair

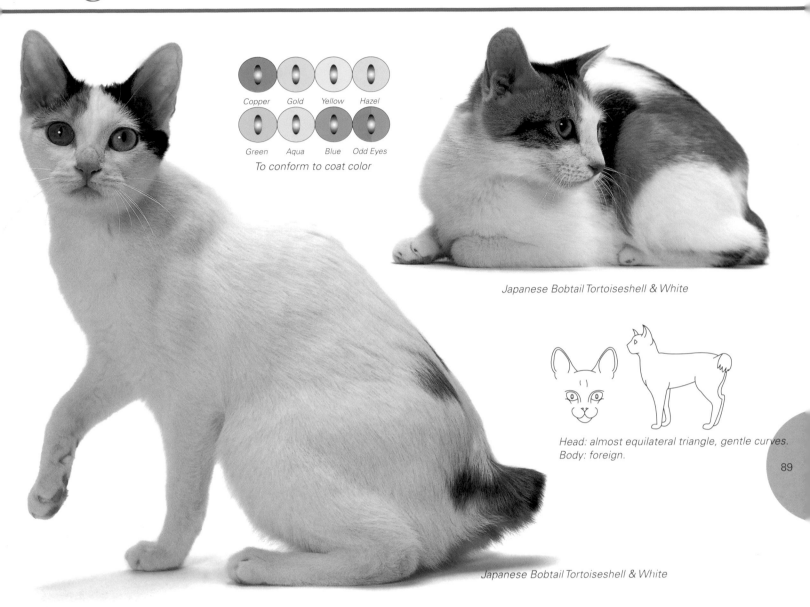

Copper Gold Yellow Hazel

Green Aqua Blue Odd Eyes

To conform to coat color

Japanese Bobtail Tortoiseshell & White

Head: almost equilateral triangle, gentle curves.
Body: foreign.

89

Japanese Bobtail Tortoiseshell & White

tively camouflages the underlying bone structure of the tail. The tail should be between two and three inches in length and may be straight, curved, or angled. The tail is peculiar not only to the breed but also to each individual cat. Like human fingerprints, no two tails are ever alike. The tail is composed of one or more curves, angles, or kinks, or any combination thereof; it may be flexible or rigid. The tailbone should extend no more than three inches from the body. The direc-

tion of the tail is not important. The tail should be of a size and shape that harmonizes with the rest of the cat.

Color and Pattern

The Japanese Bobtail is recognized in all colors of all divisions.

Traditionally, the tortoiseshell-and-white combination has been the favorite among lovers of this cat breed.

Temperament

Japanese Bobtails are strong and healthy cats. They are active, intelligent, talkative cats who enjoy the company of their fellow Japanese Bobtails and also the company of humans. They are sociable cats—that will carry on a "conversation" with their owners or fetch objects—yet they are quiet in their own way. Some owners say that, instead of meowing, these cats sing.

Pointed Color

Seal Chocolate Cinnamon Blue Lilac Fawn Red Cream

Pattern

Solid Color Tortoise-shell Agouti Tabby Mackerel Tabby Spotted Tabby Classic Tabby Silver Tipped Color Parti-Color

JAPANESE BOBTAIL LONGHAIR

The soft, silky longhaired version of the Japanese Bobtail has a
tail that looks like a powder puff.

Head: almost equilateral triangle, gentle curves.
Body: foreign.

Copper   Gold   Yellow   Hazel

Green   Aqua   Blue   Odd Eyes

To conform to coat color

Japanese Bobtail Longhair Blue Mackerel
Tabby & White

Japanese Bobtail Longhair
Red & White

Traditional Color									Sepia & Mink Color							
Black	Chocolate	Cinnamon	Blue	Lilac	Fawn	Red	Cream	White	Seal	Chocolate	Cinnamon	Blue	Lilac	Fawn	Red	Cream

*Japanese Bobtail Longhair
Black & White*

*Japanese Bobtail Longhair
Brown Torbie & White*

History

The Japanese Bobtail Longhair made its appearance in TICA in 1992. The Japanese Bobtail is a natural breed, and since these cats were living in apartments, on farms, and in the streets, they of course bred to any cat available to them. It was only natural that the longhair gene would make its presence known eventually.

Appearance

Both the Japanese Bobtail Shorthair and the Longhair are elegant and almost haughty in appearance; they hold their heads up high to show off their sculptured features. The ears are similar to those of the Akita dog: they are large, set high on the head, and pitched forward.

Color and Pattern

The Japanese Bobtail Longhair is recognized in all colors, all divisions, and all categories.

Temperament

These cats are sociable and very easy to get along with.

Pointed Color

   | Blue | Lilac | Fawn |

Seal Chocolate Cinnamon Blue Lilac Fawn Red Cream

Pattern

Solid Color | Tortoise-shell | Agouti Tabby | Mackerel Tabby | Spotted Tabby | Classic Tabby | Silver | Tipped Color | Parti-Color

Korat

The cat with the heart-shaped face and head, the Korat has
peridot green eyes and a silvery sheen to its coat.

Korat Blue

General Description

This is a small but strong cat that is
always ready to leap, like a well-coiled
spring. The jewel-like, expressive eyes
are a marvel, the color of peridot gem-
stones. Just looking at this beautiful
blue cat would give anyone goose-
bumps.

History

Legend has it that the Korat originated
in Siam (now Thailand) centuries ago,
in the court of King Rama V. The breed
was known there as Si-Sawat and was
considered a symbol of good fortune.
Si-Sawat cats were often given as treasured gifts to those held in high

esteem. The Korat was rarely sold.
Indeed, giving a pair of these cats to
newlyweds is still considered to bring
good fortune to the couple. The cats
are also reported to have guarded
homes and villages in ancient Siam.
The modern breed name is derived
from Korat, a province in northeast
Thailand. It was not until the late
1960s that the Korat arrived in North
America and Europe.

Appearance

The Korat is a shorthaired cat with a
semi-cobby body. The body is medium
sized, compact and muscular, with
strong leg boning. The legs are of mod-

Traditional Color									Sepia & Mink Color							
Black	Chocolate	Cinnamon	Blue	Lilac	Fawn	Red	Cream	White		Seal	Chocolate	Cinnamon	Blue	Lilac	Fawn	Red	Cream

Copper   Gold   Yellow   Hazel

Green   Aqua   Blue   Odd Eyes

Green only

Korat Blue in Chieng Mai, Thailand.

Head: heart shaped.
Body: semi-cobby.

93

Korat Blue

erate length, the front legs slightly shorter than the back legs. The close-lying coat is short to medium in length, glossy and fine. The heart-shaped head is formed by the prominent eyebrow ridges and an indentation between the brow ridges, which form the upper curves. The curves continue gently down to the muzzle to complete the heart. The eyes must be set well apart, fitting into the wide top part of the heart shape of the face. If the eyes are too close together, the heart shape is lost. This breed has another unique feature to the head: there is a double heart with the ears forming the top.

Color and Pattern

The Korat is shown in the solid division, traditional category, blue color only.

The cat is pale silver-blue all over, with no shading or tabby markings. Each hair should have a silver tip, giving a frosty or silvery sheen, like a halo, over the entire cat. This silver tipping seen in the Korat and the Russian Blue is not the result of the Inhibitor gene. The ends of the hair shaft are so slight that the clustered granules cannot make it all the way to the ends; therefore these tips have no pigment.

Temperament

This breed is a very sweet, patient, and loving kind of cat. The Korat is particularly good with children, as devoted to its favorite child as an Akita dog is to its owners. These cats are extremely intelligent. If you own a Korat, make sure all food containers are securely closed and put out of the cat's reach, because it will figure out how to open them. At least one Korat learned how to work electric light switches and would actually turn the lights on and off to get the owner's attention. If you plan to own a Korat, be prepared to give it the time and attention it needs. The Korat forms a very strong bond with its owner and makes a faithful and loving companion.

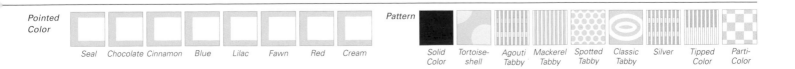

Pointed Color

Seal   Chocolate   Cinnamon   Blue   Lilac   Fawn   Red   Cream

Pattern

Solid Color   Tortoise-shell   Agouti Tabby   Mackerel Tabby   Spotted Tabby   Classic Tabby   Silver   Tipped Color   Parti-Color

La Perm

The La Perm is known as the curly-haired beauty of the cat world.

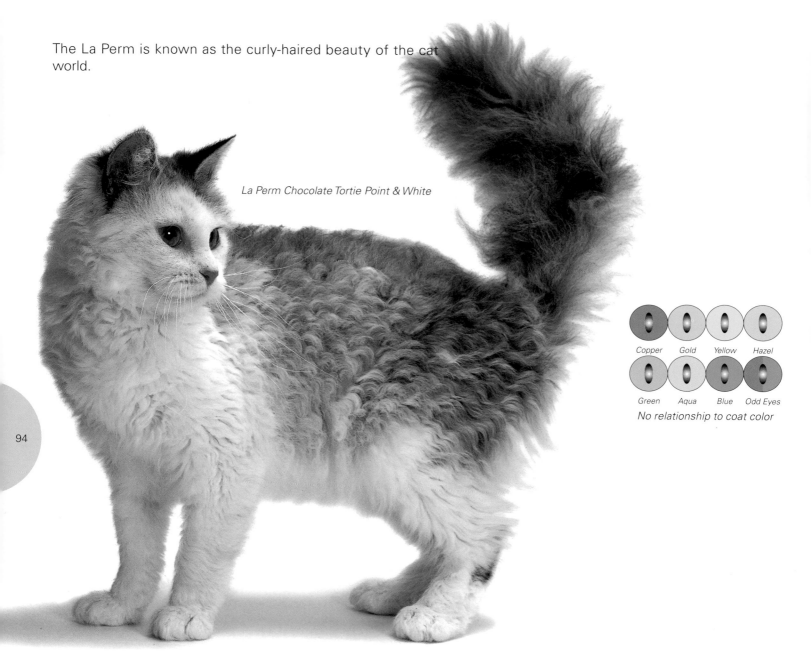

La Perm Chocolate Tortie Point & White

Copper Gold Yellow Hazel

Green Aqua Blue Odd Eyes

No relationship to coat color

General Description

The curly-coated La Perm comes in the longhair and shorthair varieties. The coat, medium length for the La Perm Shorthair and semi-long for the La Perm Longhair, is the result of a natural genetic mutation.

History

The La Perm was discovered by Linda Koehl, of Oregon, in 1982. One of her barn cats delivered a litter of kittens. Among these kittens was a different-looking one in that he was born com- pletely bald and was smaller, longer, and had bigger ears than the other kit- tens. Linda decided to keep him and gave him the name of Speedy. Within approximately eight weeks, extremely soft, curly hair started to grow. After a few years, one of Speedy's progeny wandered across the road and bred to her neighbor's shorthaired black cat. This breeding resulted in one straight- haired kitten and five curly-coated kittens. These kittens had even thicker coats than the original kitten. By breed- ing Speedy (and other La Perms) to other domestic straight-coated cats, it was determined that this curly coat came from a dominant gene and there- fore was not related to the Cornish or Devon Rex genes, which are recessive.

This breed is still being developed. The breeders first worked on getting and keeping the curly coat. They then had to work on developing the breed's distinctive physical features.

Making a new breed is not an easy task. In the past, when someone discovered a cat with a different pat- tern, hair length, or hair texture, it

Traditional Color									Sepia & Mink Color							
Black	Chocolate	Cinnamon	Blue	Lilac	Fawn	Red	Cream	White	Seal	Chocolate	Cinnamon	Blue	Lilac	Fawn	Red	Cream

Head: modified wedge with rounded contours.
Body: semi-foreign.

La Perm White

La Perm Blue Mackerel Torbie

could be introduced as a new breed. This is no longer the case. Breeders are required to prove that their new breed is completely different in type from any existing championship breed.

Appearance

The La Perm's body type is semi-foreign, with a characteristic long neck. The head is a broad modified wedge, with rounded contours. There is a slight stop between the forehead and the beginning of the nose. The muzzle should be round and prominent with a muzzle break. The cheekbones should be high. The almond-shaped eyes are large. The medium-sized ears are set moderately wide. The tightest curls are on the underside of the neck and at the base of the ears. The ear furnishings and whiskers also may be curly. Even the tail is curly. The coat requires little grooming.

Some of these cats may temporarily become bald at some point during their lives. This usually happens to the young La Perm or sometimes to females prior to their first breeding. The coat usually comes back even curlier than before; at this time, previously straight-haired La Perm kittens get their curly coat. Therefore, it is wise to wait before deciding that your straight-haired kitten is not a La Perm.

Color and Pattern

The La Perm is recognized in all colors, all divisions, and all categories. What fun it is to see these curly-coated cats in a variety of colors and patterns!

Temperament

This is a low-maintenance breed. La Perms tend to be very quiet and are only vocal when they want attention. They enjoy the company of humans and make very gentle and soothing companions.

Pointed Color

Seal Chocolate Cinnamon Blue Lilac Fawn Red Cream

Pattern

Solid Color Tortoise-shell Agouti Tabby Mackerel Tabby Spotted Tabby Classic Tabby Silver Tipped Color Parti-Color

Maine Coon

A gentle giant, the Maine Coon is one of the largest breeds of longhaired cats, with a shaggy, uneven coat, huge ears, and heavy body and feet.

General Description

The Maine Coon is a heavy, uneven-coated cat with a long, bushy tail, huge, high-set ears, and a rather wild look. The eyes, which seem to be saying "don't mess with me," have a look of quiet authority, although some may have a softened, gentle look.

History

One of the oldest natural breeds in North America's New England area, the Maine Coon has been around since the late 1800s. It is generally regarded to be a native of the state of Maine (in fact, the Maine Coon is the state cat of Maine). The Maine Coons found there were a hardy, handsome breed of domestic cat and well equipped to survive the hostile New England winters.

For the most part, planned breedings of Maine Coons have only taken place in the last forty years. In 1968, six breeders formed the Maine Coon Breeders and Fanciers Association (MCBFA) to preserve and protect the breed. Today, MCBFA membership includes over one thousand fanciers and two hundred breeders.

Some people have held the ridiculous belief that the Maine Coon

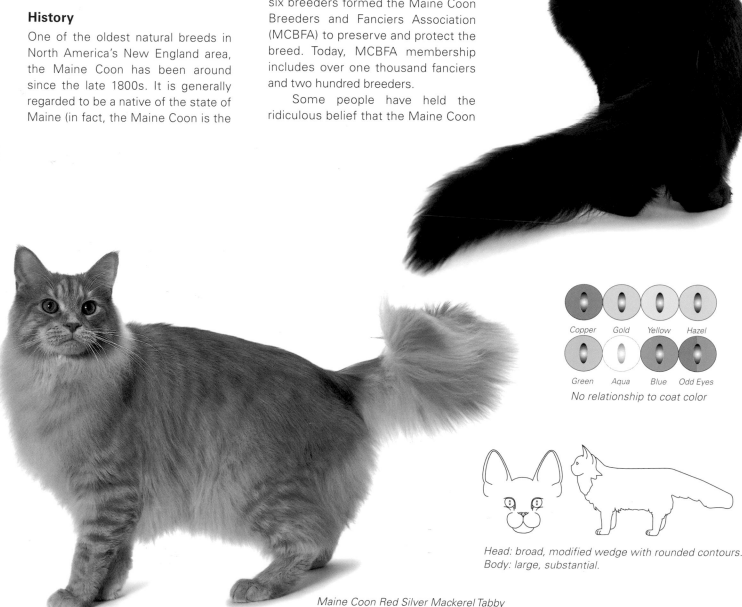

Maine Coon Black

Copper | Gold | Yellow | Hazel

Green | Aqua | Blue | Odd Eyes

No relationship to coat color

Head: broad, modified wedge with rounded contours.
Body: large, substantial.

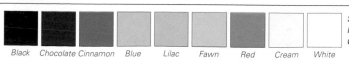

Maine Coon Red Silver Mackerel Tabby

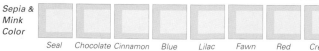

Traditional Color	Black	Chocolate	Cinnamon	Blue	Lilac	Fawn	Red	Cream	White	Sepia & Mink Color	Seal	Chocolate	Cinnamon	Blue	Lilac	Fawn	Red	Cream

Maine Coon White

Maine Coon Tortoiseshell & White

Maine Coon Brown Mackerel Tabby

Pointed Color								Pattern								
Seal	Chocolate	Cinnamon	Blue	Lilac	Fawn	Red	Cream	Solid Color	Tortoise-shell	Agouti Tabby	Mackerel Tabby	Spotted Tabby	Classic Tabby	Silver	Tipped Color	Parti-Color

Maine Coon Brown Mackerel Tabby

originated from matings between semi-wild domestic cats and raccoons. This is, of course, a genetic impossibility. Most breeders now believe that the breed resulted from matings between shorthaired domestic cats and longhaired cats from overseas. The early ancestor of the Maine Coons may have been the Norwegian Forest Cat, as it is now called, brought to the New World by the Vikings.

Maine Coons were exhibited in many of the early cat shows; a black and white Maine Coon, named Captain Jenks of the Horse Marines, was recorded in 1861 at shows in Boston and New York. Later, in 1895, a brown tabby, named Cosie, won the award for Best Cat at the Madison Square Garden Cat Show (New York City). The Maine Coon's popularity declined with

the arrival of the Persian cats in 1900. In the 1950s the breed regained its popularity. In the 1980s, the Maine Coon was recognized by all registries. Today it is one of the most popular breeds.

Appearance

The head is a broad, modified wedge with rounded contours and a broad square muzzle. The eyes are really large and oval in shape, slanting ever so slightly toward the base of the ears. The ears must be large; lynx tipping to the ears adds to the overall wild look. The standard calls for the ears to be set high on the head, with the bases being no more than an ear's width apart. The ears should not flare out.

This is one of our largest breeds of cats. The body is large, the neck is strong, and the legs and feet are

strong and substantial. The body and medium-length legs should fit into a long rectangular shape. The boning and musculature must be substantial. Females, of course, may be slightly smaller than the males. The feet are huge, with tufts of long hair growing out from between the toes. Maine Coons develop slowly, not reaching their full size until they are three to five years old.

The uneven, shaggy coat lies flat and is not full or dense. The Maine's coat does require regular combing and bathing in order to prevent it from matting. Many Maine Coons love playing with water, but some hate being bathed. Because of these cats' size and strength, some people may find it difficult to bathe one of them without help.

Maine Coon.
left: Blue Mackerel Tabby.
center: Cream Mackerel Tabby.
right: Blue Tortie.

Maine Coon Blue

Maine Coon Red Classic Tabby

Maine Coon Brown Classic Tabby & White

Maine Coon Brown Classic Torbie & White

Maine Coon Classic Tabby

Maine Coon Red Classic Tabby & White

Color and Pattern

The Maine Coon is recognized in all colors and divisions of the traditional category.

Most early Maine Coons were brown tabbies. Over time, other patterns and colors have been added, including smoke and the dominant white.

Temperament

Relaxed and easygoing, the Maine Coons generally get along well with children and dogs, as well as other cats. They are people-oriented cats, but they are not overdependent. They do not constantly demand attention, preferring to "hang out" with their owners. They do not necessarily want to be held, but they do want to be close to the person they love. In fact, some develop such a strong attachment to their female owners that they become recalcitrant when the female owner is away. Their large size belies their tiny voice—for such big cats, they are fairly quiet. Although Maine Coons are imposing in appearance and can even have a wild look about them, most are nothing but sweet cats.

My present Maine Coon, an altered female, is a calm, collected cat, controlling the household with a mere glance of the eye. The people, the furniture, even the other cats in the house are under her authority.

Maine Coon Brown Classic Tabby

Maine Coon Tortoiseshell

Manx/Cymric

The tailless breed of the cat fancy, the Manx is known as the "rabbit" cat, because it hops just like a rabbit.

General Description

Besides the lack of a tail, the Manx is known for its robust and rounded appearance. This cat can actually be drawn with a series of circles. It has a sweet expression, a very round head, and rounded cheeks, which give it a jowly appearance; this is true even more in the male cat than in the female. It is high in the hindquarters, with the back legs much longer than the forelegs, causing the rump to be higher than the shoulders. The short back forms a continuous arch from shoulders to rump. The eyes are rounded but set at a slight tilt toward the ear.

History

The origin of the Manx is not known for sure, but it is believed to have originated hundreds of years ago on the Isle of Man, off the coast of England. Ships from other countries visited the Isle for trading. Cats were absolutely essential to these ships (to keep the rodent populations down); all ships had cats. Vikings may have brought the tailless cats to the Isle of Man during the island's early colonization. Since the Vikings were great travelers, one would not know what kinds of cats were aboard or where the Vikings might have picked them up.

I believe that the genetics of the Manx, or tailless gene, is not fully understood. I also believe that all living Manx are heterozygous (M/m) for this gene and that homozygous kittens (M/M) either die in utero or, if they are born alive, are born with severe abnormalities. It has been reported that in some bloodlines, kittens appear to be healthy until they begin to eat solid food.

Appearance

The Manx displays the absolute extreme of the cobby body. The Manx and the Cymric (the Manx longhaired cousin) have the shortest, cobbiest bodies of all the breeds; the breeders, on the other hand, try to avoid breeding cats with too-short bodies. The taillessness is the result of a dominant gene that determines the length of the

| Copper | Gold | Yellow | Hazel |
| Green | Aqua | Blue | Odd Eyes |

To conform to coat color

Head: round.
Body: cobby.

Manx Blue Tortie & White

Manx Red Classic Tabby

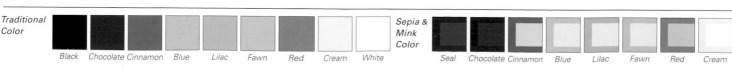

| Traditional Color | | | | | | | | | Sepia & Mink Color | | | | | | | |
| Black | Chocolate | Cinnamon | Blue | Lilac | Fawn | Red | Cream | White | | Seal | Chocolate | Cinnamon | Blue | Lilac | Fawn | Red | Cream |

Manx Black & White

Manx White

Manx Black & White

spinal column. If the spinal column is too short, kittens could be born with an open spine, weak hindquarters, or lack of control of their bowels or bladder.

Not only does the Manx have a short, compact body, but it must also have depth of flank. That is, when viewing the cat from above, the stomach area is of good size and substance. The hind legs are higher than the front legs, which give the cat an almost hopping gait. This is an extremely sturdy and strong cat.

The head is round and slightly longer than it is broad. Only a very gentle nose dip (a slight stop between the eyebrow and the beginning of the nose) should be present. The eyes should be large, round, and set at a slight angle. The Manx must also have wide-set, flared ears. When viewed from behind, the ear set is said to look like the rocker of a cradle. The shorthaired double coat should be extremely thick and plush, which adds to the compact appearance of this breed. The undercoat should be the same length as the guard hairs.

In the 1960s, in order to make sure there was no hint of a tail, judges had to put a finger in the indentation where the tail would have been. Now, the standard is a little more lenient, allowing a very slight riser.

Color and Pattern

The Manx is shown in all colors, all categories, and all divisions. This means there is the possibility of more than 350 colors and patterns; the presence of the white spotting factor would allow more than 700 possible colors and patterns.

Temperament

The Manx is a very playful cat. Due to its extremely powerful hindquarters, the Manx can jump higher and farther than one would imagine. Manx cats love high perches, and they can balance on the thinnest ledge or stand on the top of an open door. The hind legs are used for stability in situations where tailed cats would depend on the tail for balance. The Manx has been compared to a racing car, complete with rapid acceleration and an ability to make sharp turns. These cats do tend to be loyal to only one person and aloof but not unkind toward others. They make excellent, faithful companions, especially for a person living alone.

Manx Blue Tortie

Pointed Color — Seal Chocolate Cinnamon Blue Lilac Fawn Red Cream

Pattern — Solid Color Tortoise-shell Agouti Tabby Mackerel Tabby Spotted Tabby Classic Tabby Silver Tipped Color Parti-Color

CYMRIC

The Cymric is the Manx's longhaired cousin.

Head: round.
Body: cobby.

Cymric Red Classic Tabby & White

Cymric Black & White

General Description

The Cymric should be exactly like the Manx except for its long hair and silky coat texture. Like the Manx, the Cymric can be best described as rounded in appearance. The jowly appearance is enhanced by the long hair growing out from the jowls.

History

It is not known for sure if the Cymric was named after the ancient language *Cymric*. When the Romans conquered Britain, the Celtic language was spoken there. This language had two different dialects: Cymric and Gaelic.

It has been reported that the first Cymric appeared in litters of pedigreed Manx in Canada in the 1960s. In the 1970s the Canadian Cat Associations granted the Cymric championship status. TICA accepted the Cymric from its inception. CFA accepted it for championship status in 1989–90.

The 1999 TICA International Best Kitten of the Year was a Cymric by the

Traditional Color									Sepia & Mink Color							
Black	Chocolate	Cinnamon	Blue	Lilac	Fawn	Red	Cream	White	Seal	Chocolate	Cinnamon	Blue	Lilac	Fawn	Red	Cream

Copper Gold Yellow Hazel

Green Aqua Blue Odd Eyes

To conform to coat color

Cymric Black & Whites

name of MinuDeTails Ferragamo, a red classic tabby and white.

Appearance

Like the Manx, this is a cobby-bodied, tailless cat. There is no penalty, however, for a rise of bone or cartilage that does not stop the judge's hand when stroking down the back and over the rump. The flank should have greater depth than any other breed, adding much to the short, cobby appearance. The Cymric's semi-longhaired, silky-textured coat should have a soft, well-padded quality due to the longer open outer coat and thick, close undercoat.

Semi-longhaired usually means that the hair on the breeches (long fur on the hind legs), abdomen, and neck ruff will be longer than that on the torso.

Color and Pattern

The Cymric is shown in all colors, all divisions, and all categories. Add the longhaired coat to the entire inventory of colors and patterns and you have a glorious breed of cat.

Temperament

The Cymric, like the Manx, is playful, loyal, and loving to the person with whom it bonds. These cats love high perches and are surprisingly adept at jumping and balancing. As with the Manx, once the kittens get past the critical stage of development, they are as strong and healthy as any other cat. And they live a long life—fifteen years or more.

105

Cymric Red Classic Tabby & White

Pointed Color

Seal Chocolate Cinnamon Blue Lilac Fawn Red Cream

Pattern

Solid Color Tortoise-shell Agouti Tabby Mackerel Tabby Spotted Tabby Classic Tabby Silver Tipped Color Parti-Color

Munchkin

The Munchkin, a relatively new breed, is the sweet, endearing dwarf of the cat world.

Head: modified wedge, with rounded contours.
Body: semi-foreign, deep torso and short legs.

Munchkin Red Mackerel Tabby & White

Munchkin Black & White

Munchkin Chocolate & Black

Traditional Color									*Sepia & Mink Color*							
Black	Chocolate	Cinnamon	Blue	Lilac	Fawn	Red	Cream	White	Seal	Chocolate	Cinnamon	Blue	Lilac	Fawn	Red	Cream

Munchkin Seal Mink Ticked Tabby

Copper Gold Yellow Hazel

Green Aqua Blue Odd Eyes

No relationship to coat color

Munchkin Black

Munchkin Chocolate Classic Tabby & White

General Description

A Munchkin is a normal-sized cat in every way except in the shortness of the long bones in its legs, which may be as short as five inches, measured from the shoulder blade. The short legs, the result of a naturally occurring genetic mutation, do not appear to interfere with the cat's ability to run and jump.

The breeding of Munchkins has created much controversy in the cat fancy, even though its short legs are not a product of genetic engineering. Some cat lovers simply adore the Munchkin, while others believe that this cat is the result of a genetic abnormality and should never have been accepted as a new breed.

When I first saw a Munchkin, I myself had misgivings about whether it was wise to encourage a breed with such short legs. I felt sorry for the animal and could not imagine how it would manage to lead an active life. However, when I came to own one of these cats, I fell in love with her and the whole breed. My worries about her ability to leap and jump were completely unfounded—she made flying leaps, from table to desk to dresser, with no trouble at all. Outdoors, she chased bugs, leaped over logs, and even climbed trees. She instantly became a treasured pet.

History

The first Munchkin (in the United States) to be documented was discovered under a truck in Louisiana in 1983. This cat was examined and tested and was found to be healthy. When it was bred to a long-legged cat, it produced short-legged kittens—a birth not only of a litter but also of new breed of cat, the Munchkin. This breed is currently recognized by TICA in the New Breed and Color classification.

Appearance

The Munchkin, a dwarf cat, has distinctive short legs, which developed from a spontaneous autosomal (autosome: any chromosome other than the sex chromosomes) dominant mutation. Only the long bones of the legs are shortened. The legs are, of course, shorter and thicker than those of a long-legged cat. Since the Munchkin is a relatively new breed, the body type is still under discussion; semi-cobby and semi-foreign are the two types

Pointed Color

Seal Chocolate Cinnamon Blue Lilac Fawn Red Cream

Pattern

Solid Color | Tortoise-shell | Agouti Tabby | Mackerel Tabby | Spotted Tabby | Classic Tabby | Silver | Tipped Color | Parti-Color

from left: Munchkin Black & White, Blue Tortie Particolor Point, Blue Tortie & White (long-legged), and Black & White.

Munchkin Silver Mackerel Tabbies.

being considered. Because of its short legs, the Munchkin's comical walk is rather like that of a model on a runway—one foot is placed directly in front of the other, and the rear end sways from side to side.

The medium-sized head is almost an equilateral triangle, a modified wedge with rounded contours. In profile, a gentle rise is visible from the bridge of the nose to the flattened forehead above the eye ridges. The ears should be medium in size and set on the corners of the head. The large eyes are walnut-shaped, with a slight upward tilt.

Color and Pattern

The Munchkin is shown in all colors, all divisions, and all categories. The colors and patterns of the Munchkin are wonderfully varied.

Temperament

The Munchkin is a truly wonderful, extremely sweet cat. Munchkins are affectionate, and some are so cuddly that their attentions are almost excessive. These cats charm everyone they meet. They show keen interest in their surroundings, standing straight up on their hind legs and looking around to locate a lost object.

Munchkin Longhair Black & White

Munchkin Longhair Brown Mackerel Tabby & White

Norwegian Forest Cat

The Norwegian Forest Cat is a longhaired cat, native to Norway. This breed is distinguished and imposing.

Copper	Gold	Yellow	Hazel
Green	Aqua	Blue	Odd Eyes

No relationship to coat color

General Description

The magnificent Norwegian Forest Cat has a thick, heavy, all-weather coat, a huge, bushy tail, and huge, intelligent-looking, almond-shaped eyes. In Norway, to catch a glimpse of this cat in the wilderness is thought to bring good luck to the viewer. The Norwegian Forest Cat bears no resemblance to the Maine Coon or Siberian breed of cats. Each of these breeds has a look that is unique. The coat of the Norwegian Forest Cat and the Siberian is similar, but this is where the similarity stops.

History

The Norwegian Forest Cat, or Skogkatt, is a very old breed whose origin is unknown. Norse mythology speaks of a cat so huge that even the god Thor could not lift it from the ground. The goddess of love and fertility, Freya, was said to have cruised the sky in a carriage pulled by a pair of these cats. The earliest references to cats that resemble today's Forest Cats are found in Norwegian folk tales gathered and recorded between 1837 and 1852. It is clear, however, that these cats existed much earlier.

Norwegian Forest Cats developed the necessary attributes for survival in wintry conditions: a heavy double coat; sturdy bones; long hind legs and strong claws for swift running, jumping, and climbing. These traits enhanced their hunting ability and allowed them to be comfortable in the snow, in a tree, or on rocky terrain. Similar circumstances were to be found in Russia, where the Siberian cat inhabited the beautiful but very, very cold woods. These breeds share

Norwegian Forest Cat Brown Mackerel Tabby & White

Traditional Color	Black	Chocolate	Cinnamon	Blue	Lilac	Fawn	Red	Cream	White	Sepia & Mink Color	Seal	Chocolate	Cinnamon	Blue	Lilac	Fawn	Red	Cream

Norwegian Forest Cat Brown Mackerel Tabby & White

Norwegian Forest Cat Silver Mackerel Tabby & White

characteristics, including extremely thick coats, a strong constitution, and a good survival instinct.

In the mid-1930s a few Norwegian cat fanciers joined together to promote the Forest Cat, which in Norway is called the Skogkatt. A Skogkatt was exhibited at a show in Oslo in 1938. World War II delayed the breed's progress in the cat fancy. The Norwegian National Association of Pedigree Cats was founded in 1963, and at that time some Skogkatt fanciers began seriously working for its recognition as a pedigreed breed. A brown and white mackerel tabby Skogkatt was the first to be examined by members of the Breeding Council

at that time, and it became the prototype of the Norwegian Forest Cat breed.

The first breeding pair of Norwegian Forest Cats arrived in the United States on November 1, 1979. The first U.S.-born Norwegian Forest Cat litter arrived on March 21, 1981. In August 1984 TICA became the first North American registry to grant championship status to the Norwegian Forest Cat, which is currently accepted for championship competition by ACFA, CFA, CCA, and CFF.

Appearance

The TICA standard for the Norwegian Forest Cat requires that the cat have

large, wide-set, almond-shaped eyes. The head should fit into a straight-lined equilateral triangle. The muzzle should be pleasingly round but should fit into the straight lines of the wedge. In the profile, a straight line should stretch from the forehead to the tip of the nose. The medium to large ears are set well apart and should have heavy ear furnishings (long hairs) that can extend from the front to the back of the ear. Long, lynx-like tufts at the top of the ears complete the look of a cat that

Head: triangular.
Body: large, substantial, moderately long.

Norwegian Forest Cat Brown Classic Tabby & White

Pointed Color								Pattern								
Seal	Chocolate	Cinnamon	Blue	Lilac	Fawn	Red	Cream	Solid Color	Tortoise-shell	Agouti Tabby	Mackerel Tabby	Spotted Tabby	Classic Tabby	Silver	Tipped Color	Parti-Color

lives among the trees, in the forest.

The body should be of substantial build and there should be good depth of flank. The males will be considerably heavier and larger-boned than the females. The tail is bushy and full and resembles the tail of a skunk.

The layers of hair make the cat appear to be larger than it is. The fur protects the cat against wind and cold, and it also acts as a raincoat. Water will "bead up" on the fur, since it is a naturally oily coat. Bathing one of these cats is no small task, requiring lots of time, patience, soap, and water. The Norwegian needs as many as three applications of shampoo to make a lather in order to get down to the undercoat. However, many Norwegians keep themselves clean, so bathing may not be necessary. It is best not to bathe a Norwegian immediately before a show, since its hair will fluff up like a Persian's coat.

Color and Pattern
The Norwegian Forest Cat is recognized in all traditional colors and divisions.

Norwegian Forest Cat Brown Classic Tabby & White

Norwegian Forest Cat Silver Mackerel Torbie

Norwegian Forest Cat Black & White

Temperament

The Norwegian Forest Cat is what I call a *definite* cat. These beauties know exactly what they are doing, why they are doing it, and how to get it done. They are by nature freethinking, yet because they have been domesticated, they remain extraordinary astute, affectionate, and loving. They are usually very quiet, so it may be difficult to know when the female is in season. Most are not interested in playing games but will quietly watch other cats at play. These cats are intelligent, dependable, and sensible. When outdoors they will come when called, and they enjoy walking along with their owner as a dog would, chasing squirrels, and running up trees. With delight they bring in prizes from the outdoors—a leaf, a live mouse, or even a small garden snake—and deposit them in a special place in the house.

Norwegian Forest Cat Brown Mackerel Tabby & White

Norwegian Forest Cat Brown Mackerel Tabby & White

Norwegian Forest Cat Brown Classic Torbie & White

Norwegian Forest Cat Brown Mackerel Tabby

Norwegian Forest Cat.
left: Brown Mackerel Tabby & White.
right: Brown Classic Tabby & White.

Ocicat

The man-made Ocicat is the spotted, shorthaired athlete of the cat world.

Ocicat Brown Spotted Tabby

General Description

The Ocicat is a large, well-spotted cat of moderate type. It displays the look of an athletic animal, well muscled and solid, graceful and lithe, yet with a fullness of body and chest. This is a man-made breed, combining the Siamese, Abyssinian, and American Shorthair.

History

Virginia Daly was experimenting with a breeding program. She wanted to put the agouti tabby pattern on her lynx point Siamese by crossing Abyssinian and Siamese. The kittens of the first generation were all agouti tabbies. She took one of the females from this first generation and bred her (1964) to a chocolate point Siamese. This breeding produced a beautiful spotted kitten and was given the name of Tonga. Virginia Daly's daughter remarked that he looked like a baby Ocelot (hence their name). He was sold as a pet and neutered. When Tonga's parents produced more lovely spotted kittens, Mrs. Daly and a few other breeders began a serious breeding program for Ocicats.

Later, the American Shorthair was added into the breed, adding the silver varieties and doubling the number of Ocicat colors. Today, breeders of Ocicats no longer use the Siamese or American Shorthair. Since 1986, only

Ocicat Blue Spotted Tabby

Head: modified wedge.
Body: semi-foreign.

Traditional Color										Sepia & Mink Color							
	Black	Chocolate	Cinnamon	Blue	Lilac	Fawn	Red	Cream	White		Seal	Chocolate	Cinnamon	Blue	Lilac	Fawn	Red	Cream

Copper · Gold · Yellow · Hazel
Green · Aqua · Blue · Odd Eyes

No relationship to coat color

left: Ocicat Chocolate Spotted Tabby.
right: Ocicat Chocolate Spotted Tabby

Ocicat Brown Spotted Tabby

the Abyssinian has been permitted for use in outcrossing to improve type and enlarge the gene pool.

Appearance

The head is a modified wedge with gentle contours. The muzzle should be well defined and almost square (but not as square as the muzzle of the Maine Coon or American Shorthair). The ears are moderately large and set on the corners of the head. The large, almond-shaped eyes are slightly angled toward the ears. The neck is arched. The body is semi-foreign, large, and substantial. The coat is fine and close lying but long enough to carry several bands of ticking.

Color and Pattern

Ocicats are shown in the traditional category, tabby and silver divisions, spotted pattern and eumelanistic colors only.

In other words, the spotted tabby pattern colors (not silvered) are brown, chocolate, cinnamon, blue, lilac, and fawn. The silver spotted colors are silver, blue silver, chocolate silver, cinnamon silver, lilac silver, and fawn silver.

Temperament

While the Ocicat may look a little wild, its temperament is anything but ferocious. In fact, these cats are completely domestic animals, right down to their genes. They are very friendly, loving, outgoing cats that make excellent companions for everyone in the family, including children, dogs, and other cats. Alert and active, they are intelligent and can be taught to respond to voice commands and seem to enjoy performing tricks.

Ocicat Chocolate Spotted Tabby

Pointed Color								Pattern								
Seal	Chocolate	Cinnamon	Blue	Lilac	Fawn	Red	Cream	Solid Color	Tortoise-shell	Agouti Tabby	Mackerel Tabby	Spotted Tabby	Classic Tabby	Silver	Tipped Color	Parti-Color

With its magnificent mane and long, flowing hair, the Persian is known as the aristocrat of the cat fancy.

Persian Silver Mackerel Tabby

General Description

The combination of long, flowing hair, a massive, round head, a cobby body, and huge eyes gives this breed its distinctive look. The huge eyes, the turned-up nose, and the high cheekbones contribute to the sweet facial expression and give it a "baby doll" appearance. These features have made the Persian the number one breed in some cat-exhibition halls.

History

Persians have been shown as a recognized breed for more than one hundred years. The exact origin of the Persian is unknown. By some accounts the Persian, and other longhaired cats, may have originated from wild cats in Asia and Russia. It has also been reported that the Persian originated in Asia Minor and was first seen in Europe in the early 1700s. Other reports place longhaired cats, imported from Asia, in Italy in the late 1500s.

Did the Persian descend from the Turkish Angora? Maybe so. Early British books referred to the cats we now call Persians as French cats or Angoras; these were reported to have come from Ankara, Turkey (also the birthplace of the Turkish Angora, to which the "French cats" or "Angoras" bore a resemblance). The Turkish Angora, which appears to be behind many of the present-day breeds, was used in many breeding programs for its beautiful, long coat.

The Persians were first exhibited in Great Britain in 1871. The colors shown were black, blue, and white. The blue Persians were favored at this show. Queen Victoria and members of Britain's royal family kept blue Persians, which only added to the cat's popularity.

Angoras and Persians were shown in North America in the late 1800s. The Persian was described as different from the Angora in "the quality of its fur." Helen M. Winslow provided a general description of the Persian cat of the time in her book *Concerning Cats: My Own and Some Others* (Boston: Lothrop Publishing Company, 1900):

"The Persian cat of very great value is all black, with a very fluffy frill, or lord mayor's chain, and orange eyes. Next to him comes a light slate or blue Persian, with yellow eyes. The fur of the Persian cat is much more woolly than that of the Angora. The Angora's tail comes out thin, silky, and narrow, although it immediately 'fluffs' up. The Persian's tail does not compress itself readily into a small space. The Persian cat's head is larger, its ears are less pointed, although it should have the tuft at the end and the long hair inside. It is usually larger in body and apparently stronger made, although slender and elegant in appearance, with small bones and graceful in movement. The colors vary, as with the Angora, except that the tortoise-shell and the dark-marked tabby do not so frequently appear. The temper is usually less reliable and the intelligence less keen than the Angora."

The Persian of the past does not even closely resemble the Persian of today. The earlier Persians had longer

Traditional Color										Sepia & Mink Color							
Black	Chocolate	Cinnamon	Blue	Lilac	Fawn	Red	Cream	White			Seal	Chocolate	Cinnamon	Blue	Lilac	Fawn	Red	Cream

Copper | Gold | Yellow | Hazel
Green | Aqua | Blue | Odd Eyes

To conform to coat color

Persian Red

Head: broad, rounded, domed.
Body: cobby.

Persian Shaded Silver

Persian Black

faces, larger ears, smaller, more close-set eyes, and rangier, longer bodies. In fact, in North America in the 1800s, it was often difficult to tell a Persian from an Angora or a Maine Coon. All three had long hair, and they all had a long head and long body. At that time, cats were judged primarily on color and pattern.

Until the late 1960s, Persians in North America retained their longer muzzles, with a stop. The extreme Persians were the Peke Face. The Peke Face Persian resembled the face of a Pekinese dog, with large eyes, cascading folds of skin from under the eyes to the chin, and a turned-up nose.

They could only be shown in red or cream; any other color showing a Peke Face was automatically disqualified from exhibition. Gradually, over time, the look of the Persian changed. The head grew broader; the eyes became larger and rounder; the nose, instead of turning down, began to turn up; and the body became more compact.

The Persian, Himalayan, and Exotic Shorthair share a common standard and type. The only difference between these breeds is coat length, texture, and color. When the cat fancy got into full swing, only a small number of breeds were recognized. So when a longhair or a color variation showed up,

the cat fancy gave it a "designer" breed name, as with the Himalayan—which is actually a pointed Persian. Next was the Exotic Shorthair, which is really a shorthaired Persian.

Appearance

This is a majestic cat. The head should be round and massive with great breadth of skull. The face should be round, with a sweet expression. The jaws are to be broad and powerful. The cheeks should be prominent. The short turned-up nose should be almost as broad as it is long, with a definite break in the plane between the eyes. You should be able to put your finger in

Pointed Color

Seal | Chocolate | Cinnamon | Blue | Lilac | Fawn | Red | Cream

Pattern

Solid Color | Tortoise-shell | Agouti Tabby | Mackerel Tabby | Spotted Tabby | Classic Tabby | Silver | Tipped Color | Parti-Color

Persian Black Smoke

the indentation. The ears should be small, round, and spaced far apart. The eyes should be large, round, and wide set. The cobby body shows a deep chest, is massive across the shoulders and rump, with a short, well-rounded abdomen. The back should be level. The tail should be short (in proportion to the body) and carried at an angle lower than the back, but it should not be curved or trailing. The coat should be long all over the body. The ruff should be immense and continue in a deep frill between the front legs. Seasonal variations in coat are recognized.

Persians have a thick undercoat, which gives the coat its luxurious plushness, but it also makes the hair susceptible to matting. These cats need to be combed and brushed on a regular basis in order to prevent the hair from tangling and matting. Their long, flowing coats require a protected indoor environment. The blue Persian is especially prone to matting and must be groomed regularly. All Persians need frequent bathing (after a thorough combing), but those with white fur especially need constant cleaning in order to prevent eye stains from marring the appearance of the face.

Color and Pattern

The Persian is shown in all colors and all divisions of the traditional, sepia, and mink categories. The pointed variety is called a Himalayan.

Temperament

Persians are, for the most part, laid-back cats. Although some Persians may have sudden burst of energy and will romp and frolic just like other breeds, most are happiest when lounging and being decorative. Playful but never demanding, they love to pose and will drape themselves in a favorite window or chair, enhancing the decor, as would a treasured work of art. Persians have short, heavy-boned legs, needed to support their broad, short bodies. They like to have their feet firmly planted on the ground and are not given to high jumping and climbing. Their sweet, gentle personalities fit into most households, provided they feel secure in their environment. Creatures of habit, they are most comfortable in an atmosphere of security and serenity, but with love and reassurance they can easily adapt to the most boisterous of households. Their quiet, melodious voices are pleasant and nonabrasive. Persians make charming pets for people of all ages; their companionship is close and enduring.

Persian White

Persian Tortoiseshell & White

Persian Chinchilla Golden

HIMALAYAN

The Himalayan is a pointed Persian.

Copper   Gold   Yellow   Hazel

Green   Aqua   Blue   Odd Eyes

To conform to coat color

Himalayan Seal Point

General Description

The Himalayan should resemble a Persian in body type, coat length, and coat texture. Its pointed pattern and blue eyes give this cat distinction and individuality.

History

The Himalayan is a man-made breed created by breeding Siamese to Persian cats. The idea for the Himalayan may be traced to a geneticist in Sweden in 1922, who set about to introduce the pointed allele into the Persian gene pool. As far as we know, he bred long-haired whites with Siamese, but whether his attempt was successful is not known.

In the 1930s, American geneticists conducted research of the inheritance of the pointed gene. They bred Siamese with smoke, silver tabby, and black Persians, producing several shorthaired kittens. Two of these kittens were mated to produce a long-haired black female, which was mated to her sire. This mating produced the first longhaired pointed kitten, born in 1935 and named Debutante. Although Debutante could be considered the first Himalayan, she had a foreign body type. Indeed, it took many, many years to produce the show-quality, Persian-type Himalayan that we know today.

The Himalayan made its public debut in the 1950s, and in 1955 it was

recognized as a breed and given a breed number, as a Color Point Longhair. By the 1960s, all cat organizations recognized them as a separate breed.

Appearance

The pointed, blue-eyed Himalayan, so like the Persian in body, coat length, and texture, should be gentle and amenable to being handled, while giving the impression of robust power. The chest should be deep and equally massive across the shoulders and rump. The expression should be sweet, never frowning in appearance. The nose, like the Persian's, should have an upward turn. The head should

Traditional Color									Sepia & Mink Color							
Black	Chocolate	Cinnamon	Blue	Lilac	Fawn	Red	Cream	White	Seal	Chocolate	Cinnamon	Blue	Lilac	Fawn	Red	Cream

Himalayan Seal Tortie Point

Himalayan Blue Point

Himalayan Seal Tortie Point

Himalayan Red Point

Head: broad, rounded, domed.
Body: cobby.

123

Pointed Color								
Seal	Chocolate	Cinnamon	Blue	Lilac	Fawn	Red	Cream	

Pattern								

Solid Color	Tortoise-shell	Agouti Tabby	Mackerel Tabby	Spotted Tabby	Classic Tabby	Silver	Tipped Color	Parti-Color

Himalayan Seal Point

Himalayan Red Point

be round and broad with small, wide-set ears. Its huge, round, blue eyes should make a striking contrast against its pointed mask color. The long, flowing coat needs the same constant combing and bathing as that of the Persian.

Color and Pattern

The Himalayan is recognized in all pointed colors and patterns in the pointed category.

The particolor points were added to the list of accepted colors several years ago, despite the fact that this breed could now have the white spotting gene and could possibly have the Van pattern whereas there could be only a spot of color on the top of the head. If this pattern were to occur, it would certainly not fit the color description of the Himalayan. However, the Himalayan breeders in TICA argued that since they were allowed to breed freely with the Exotic and Persian, which already had the white spotting gene, a particolor point pattern could be a natural genetic outcome.

Temperament

The Himalayan, like the Persian, tends to be a gentle, relaxed cat. These cats are so appealing as to elicit extra affection from their owners. What could be prettier than a cat with long hair, a light body color, darker points (the extremities of the cat), and heavenly blue eyes? The Himalayan, like its Persian cousin, may have occasional sudden bursts of energy.

124

Himalayan Blue Lynx Point

Himalayan Seal Point

Himalayan Blue Point

EXOTIC SHORTHAIR

The Exotic Shorthair is a Persian cat with a shorthaired coat.

Exotic Shorthair Red Mackerel Tabby

General Description

The Exotic Shorthair is a Persian with a short, plush coat. This cat has been nicknamed "the lazy man's Persian" and "the no-upkeep Persian." The Exotic Shorthair is a wonderful pet for those who love the Persian's beauty but prefer to avoid the hours and hours of arduous grooming.

History

In the early 1960s, the Exotic Shorthair (a man-made breed) was introduced to the cat fancy by American breeders. They bred the Persian with the American Shorthair in an attempt to produce a Persian type with short hair. The campaign to have the Exotic Shorthair recognized by cat organizations was met by outrage on the part of some Persian breeders. They were needlessly afraid that, once the shorthair gene was introduced into the gene pool, their Persians would produce Exotic Shorthairs. This is not genetically possible, as a longhaired cat (result of recessive genes *l/l*) could not ever produce a shorthaired (dominant gene *L/−*) cat. Eventually, through perseverance, the Exotic Shorthair breed was recognized for championship competition.

Some organizations have had trouble deciding where to place longhaired cats that are produced from Exotic breedings. In some organizations they are called Longhaired Exotics. TICA registers them as Exotic Shorthair variants and places them with the Persians (since they *are* Persians).

Appearance

The Exotic Shorthair is just like the Persian, except for its coat, which is short, dense, and plush. Exotic Shorthair breeders are particular about the length and texture of their cats' coats. The guard hairs should not be too long, otherwise the coat will drape down. There should be an abundance of undercoat. Exotics have been called "Persians in pajamas," because unlike the Persian, whose faults may be disguised under long hair, with the Exotic what you see is what you get.

Color and Pattern

Exotic Shorthairs are shown in all colors, all divisions, and all categories in TICA, including sepia, mink, and the pointed colors.

Exotic Shorthair Black

Traditional Color									Sepia & Mink Color							
Black	Chocolate	Cinnamon	Blue	Lilac	Fawn	Red	Cream	White	Seal	Chocolate	Cinnamon	Blue	Lilac	Fawn	Red	Cream

Exotic Shorthair Tortoiseshell & White

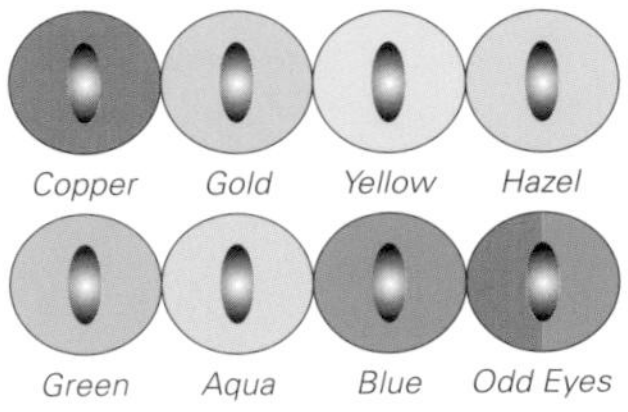

Copper Gold Yellow Hazel

Green Aqua Blue Odd Eyes

To conform to coat color

127

Exotic Shorthair Blue Silver Classic Tabby

Head: broad, rounded, domed.
Body: cobby.

Exotic Shorthair Brown Mackerel Torbie

Temperament

The Exotic Shorthairs are quiet, relaxed cats. They are a soft, sweet, and peaceful breed of cat, possessing qualities of the Persian, Burmese, British Shorthair, and American Shorthair. Nothing seems to ruffle them, and they take life in stride. Many of these teddy-bear-like cats are affectionate lap-sitters, yet they will give you privacy when you need it and will not make excessive demands. They may, however, like their Persian cousins, be taken over by sudden bursts of energy and enter into serious play.

Pointed
Color

Seal   Chocolate Cinnamon   Blue   Lilac   Fawn   Red   Cream

Pattern

Solid
Color

Tortoise-
shell

Agouti
Tabby

Mackerel
Tabby

Spotted
Tabby

Classic
Tabby

Silver

Tipped
Color

Parti-
Color

Pixiebob

Its signature is a muted spotted tabby pattern, a short tail, and a wild, wild look.

Pixiebob Brown Spotted Tabby

Traditional Color	Black	Chocolate	Cinnamon	Blue	Lilac	Fawn	Red	Cream	White	Sepia & Mink Color	Seal	Chocolate	Cinnamon	Blue	Lilac	Fawn	Red	Cream

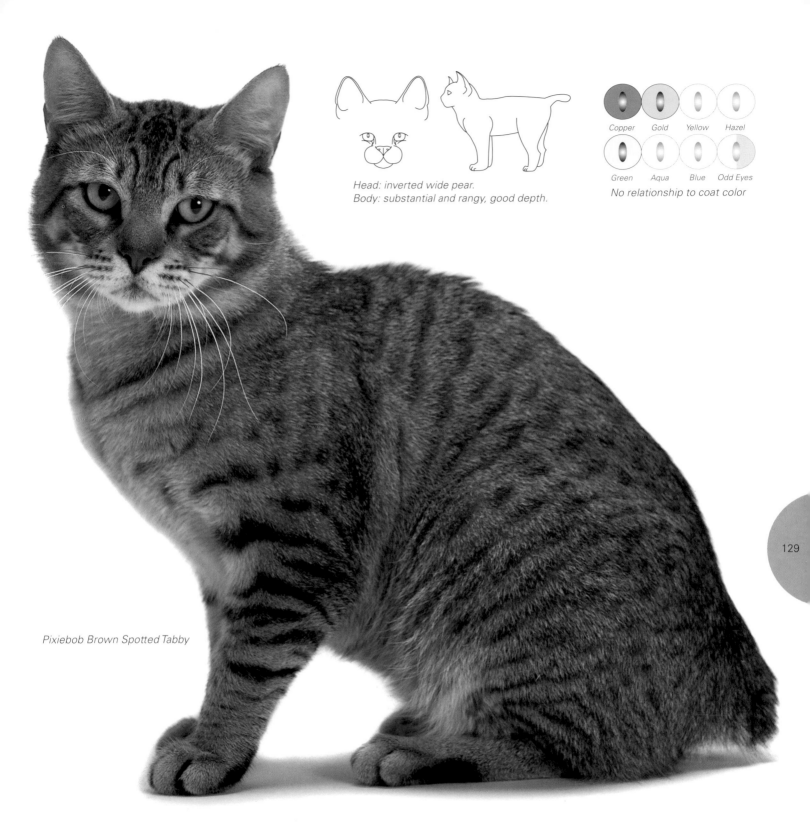

Head: inverted wide pear.
Body: substantial and rangy, good depth.

Copper Gold Yellow Hazel
Green Aqua Blue Odd Eyes
No relationship to coat color

Pixiebob Brown Spotted Tabby

General Description

The Pixiebob, a relatively new breed, is a domestic cat bred to have the visual appearance of the North American Bobcat. There is currently no proof that the Pixiebob has the Bobcat as its ancestor; this is a domestic cat. The Pixiebob has a "wild" look to the face, mutton chops, and a thick, thick coat with distinctive ticking and spots. This big, strong cat with a short tail comes in both the longhair and shorthair varieties.

History

In 1985, a classic tabby cat with large feet, a large head, and a short tail was found on Mt. Baker in Washington State and given to breeder Carol Brewer (founder of the breed). Carol decided to attempt to breed a domestic cat that looked like a Bobcat. The next year, Carol obtained Maggie, a small, spotted tabby, fawn-colored female cat with almost no tail and a "wild" look to her face, and her female kitten, named Pixie. Carol bought a male kitten that had the look she desired and named him Sasha. Pixie and Sasha were the foundation cats of the Pixiebob breed. They produced the magnificent male kitten Bobby

Pointed Color

Seal Chocolate Cinnamon Blue Lilac Fawn Red Cream

Pattern

Solid Color Tortoise-shell Agouti Tabby Mackerel Tabby Spotted Tabby Classic Tabby Silver Tipped Color Parti-Color

Pixiebob Brown Spotted Tabby

Woodruff, who is still seen in cat shows.

The Pixiebob breed was registered with TICA as an experimental breed in October 1994, and in September 1995 the breed was accepted for showing in the NBC class (new breed or color). In May 1998 the Pixiebob was advanced to championship status in TICA. These cats are now competing alongside other established breeds.

Appearance

The Pixiebob is a large, muscular, rangy cat with heavy bone structure and loose skin, standing a little higher in the back legs, with a short tail (two to six inches long) and large feet. If the cat is a polydactyl (extra toes), the feet are much larger. The Pixiebob standard is the only standard that accepts the polydactyls. Males usually weigh fourteen to eighteen pounds, and females weigh ten to twelve pounds. The Pixiebob has deep-set eyes and heavy brows, with a "worried" look. The ears should be large, and lynx tipping is preferred. This cat should have a distinct muzzle and a very strong chin.

The brown spotted, double coat stands out away from the body, rather than lying flat. The coat on the short-haired Pixiebob is short and extremely thick, yet it is not plush like that of the British Shorthair. The coat of the long-haired cat is equally grand, emphasizing the mutton chops. The ticking is not the refined variety seen on other championship cats; it is more like the agouti ticking of a wild animal.

Color and Pattern

The Pixiebob is recognized in the traditional category, tabby division, in the brown spotted tabby pattern only.

The spotting pattern, muted with heavy ticking like that of a wild hare, consists of small spots, with or without rosettes. The guard hairs on the top of the back may be black and coarse.

Temperament

Although wild in appearance, Pixiebobs are domestic in nature. These intelligent, inquisitive cats are dog-like in their devotion and loyalty and are easily trained to walk on a leash. They usually form a strong bond with their family and make excellent companions for children. They are extremely quiet, uttering only an occasional chirp or chatter. Pixiebobs enjoy scratching on a piece of wood and are very clean in their litter-box habits. The owners of Pixiebobs swear by these loving, delightful cats; some say that owning a Pixiebob is a very serious addiction—one is not enough!

Pixiebob Brown Spotted Tabby

Pixiebob Longhair Brown Spotted Tabby

Pixiebob Longhair Brown Spotted Tabby

Ragdoll

One of the largest breeds of cats, the Ragdoll is a pointed, semi-longhaired cat with a tendency to become limp when it is picked up.

| Copper | Gold | Yellow | Hazel |
| Green | Aqua | Blue | Odd Eyes |

Blue only

General Description

The Ragdoll, named for its tendency to go floppy when picked up, is one big, lovable bundle of silky fur. The cat is a striking combination of dark points, light body color, and beautiful China-blue eyes.

History

The exact circumstances of the Ragdoll's origin are unknown. The following is how the stories go; fact or fiction, I do not know.

There are, however, several repeats that appear in most of the histories.

Josephine, an "Angora-type" long-haired almost feral cat, was owned by Mrs. Pennels, apparently a neighbor of Ann Baker.

Ann Baker, in the early 1960s, was the originator of the Ragdoll.

Josephine may have been bred to a male that resembled a Birman, producing a cat Ann Baker called Raggedy Ann Daddy Warbucks.

First history:

In the 1960s, either Mrs. Pennels or Ann Baker of Riverside, California, rescued a cat (Josephine) that had been hit by a car. Josephine received head injuries that changed her personality and made her immune to pain—she suddenly became very laid-back and "floppy." This trait she was to pass on to her kittens. Fact or fiction? Most geneticists would say that this is completely impossible. It should be noted that the present-day Ragdoll is not impervious to pain, as Ann Baker led the early owners of Ragdolls to believe.

Second history:

Ann Baker bred Josephine to a seal point Birman. One of the male offspring was then bred to a female Burmese. Some people believe this to be the foundation for the Ragdoll.

Third history:

Josephine had five or six kittens; two of the males (Blackie and Warbucks) were loaned to Ann Baker to be used in her breeding program. These male kittens had different sires.

Ragdoll Seal Lynx Point

Ragdoll Blue Tortie Point Mitted

132

Traditional Color									Sepia & Mink Color							
Black	Chocolate	Cinnamon	Blue	Lilac	Fawn	Red	Cream	White		Seal	Chocolate	Cinnamon	Blue	Lilac	Fawn	Red	Cream

Head: modified wedge with rounded contours.
Body: long and substantial.

Ragdoll Chocolate Point Bicolor

Ragdoll Blue Point Bicolor

Fourth history:

Ragdolls are supposedly descended from three cats:

Josephine—Persian/Angora-type cat appears to be the mother of them all.

Blackie—a black/brown Persian and son of Josephine. This cat was loaned to Ann Baker to breed to her own Persian females.

Raggedy Ann Daddy Warbucks—Blackie's brother, a white-mitted male (a cat resembling a Birman) and son of Josephine by an unknown father. This cat was loaned to Ann Baker to breed to her own Persian females.

Ann Baker began breeding "Ragdolls" and would often hire other people to help her in the breeding program. In the 1970s she developed her own registry for them, which she named the International Ragdoll Cat Association (IRCA). Cats registered in IRCA could not be registered or shown in other cat associations.

In the 1970s, a group of Ragdoll breeders broke off from the original group and worked hard to have the Ragdoll accepted for registration in other registries. These breeders proceeded to breed the Ragdoll according to their own goals for the breed's appearance. These dedicated breeders took it upon themselves to refine and define the breed's type, while maintaining the desired white spotting pattern. Their work resulted in the grand, stately Ragdoll of today.

Appearance

The Ragdoll is a semi-longhaired pointed cat with a long and substantial body and a sweet and docile disposition. The ideal Ragdoll grows exceptionally large and heavy. Full weight and size are not reached until the cat is at least four years old. Full development of color is not achieved until two years of age.

The head is a broad, modified wedge, with slightly rounded contours, ending with a rounded, well-developed muzzle and chin. The medium-sized ears are broad at the base, rounded at the tip, and form a continuation of the

Pointed Color

Seal Chocolate Cinnamon Blue Lilac Fawn Red Cream

Pattern

Solid Color Tortoise-shell Agouti Tabby Mackerel Tabby Tabby (Lynx) Classic Tabby Silver Tipped Color Parti-Color

modified wedge. The moderately wide-set large oval eyes must be blue. The legs are substantial, medium in length, with large, round, tufted feet. The chest is broad and full, and the body should be firm with no fat except on the lower abdomen. The adult Ragdoll has a tendency toward a fatty pad on the lower abdomen. The tail is long and full.

The plush and silky coat is easy to care for, since it sheds only slightly and it rarely mats. The coat is so thick that it "breaks" as the cat moves. The coat is longest on the sides of the face and around the neck, forming a bib or ruff that sets off the regal head. The hair is also long on the sides and stomach, and on the hind legs, where it forms thick "feathers."

Ragdoll Blue Point Mitted

Color and Pattern

The Ragdoll is recognized in all pointed colors of the pointed category, in the following divisions: solid point, lynx point, tortie point; all pointed colors and white particolor point division (mitted and bicolor patterns).

The Ragdoll standard has many restrictions (too numerous to write about in this book) as to the exact placement of white on the particolor point.

Temperament

Ragdolls are calm, docile, quiet cats; they are easy to handle and even easier to love. They are a friendly, affectionate, and intelligent breed of cat, and they truly love human company. Ragdolls usually show little or no interest in the great outdoors and therefore are perfect for house, apartment, and even RV living. It is indeed fortunate that they have such a sweet disposition, because male Ragdolls can reach twenty or more pounds.

Ragdoll Seal Point Bicolor

Ragdoll Seal Point Bicolor

Ragamuffin

In the late 1980s, a group of breeders broke away from IRCA and decided to give their version of the Ragdoll the name of Ragamuffin. These cats were descended from the original Ragdolls, but were bred to Persians, Himalayans, and domestic cats, as well as traditional Ragdolls, thus bringing in traditional colors (solid, tabby, tortie, silver, smoke, as well as the pointed and particolor point pattern).

The Ragamuffin is said to be similar to the Ragdoll in type but as the breeders have outcrossed to other breeds, the type is not exactly the same as the Ragdoll.

The head is a broad modified wedge with rounded contours. The whisker pads are puffy. The body is long with a solid feel to it. The long tail is fully plumed. This is a very friendly and laid back attractive cat of many colors and patterns.

Ragamuffin Seal Point Bicolor

Russian Blue/Nebelung

With its mysterious "Mona Lisa" smile and its silver-tipped hair, the rare, shorthaired Russian Blue may be the ancestor of some of today's blue-haired cats.

General Description

The Russian Blue, a foreign-type cat with a long body and legs, is noted for its soft, lustrous, bright-blue double coat and its deep, brilliant green eye color. Handling a Russian Blue feels like running a silk scarf through your hands. The coat, an even blue color, is short, thick, and very fine; its density causes the double-textured coat to stand out from the body. The silver tipping of the guard hairs gives the cat an overall lustrous silvery sheen.

History

The first Russian Blue cats are said to have originated from the Baltic port of Archangel, just outside the Arctic Circle. They were carried as trade goods by merchant ships trading with England in the mid-1800s. The Russian Blue has been called by many names over the course of its history, including Archangel, Russian Shorthair, Spanish Blue, Russian Shorthair, and Maltese Blue.

The early Russian Blues had orange eye color and were cobby in body and somewhat rounded-head. During and after World War II, the Russian Blue (like so many other breeds) nearly became extinct in Europe. In order to reestablish the Russian Blue, the breeders turned to what was available to them at that time. In this case, it was the Siamese. As a result, the Russian Blue became longer in all aspects, and finer boned; eye color changed from orange to green.

In early cat shows, all shorthaired blue cats competed in one class, regardless of type. In 1912, however, the Russian Blue was given its status as a separate breed. Eventually breeders made a collective attempt to return to the prewar characteristics of the breed. In 1965 the show standard was changed to specifically state that Siamese type was undesirable in the Russian Blue. The Russian Blues, however, still retain their foreign body type, at least in North America.

An ancient Russian fairy tale tells of seven fairies who gathered around the cradle of a newborn princess and presented their gifts. These were gifts of courage, beauty, loyalty, grace, friendship, fine clothes, and two brilliant emeralds. However, these fairies were rather young and inexperienced,

Russian Blue Blue

Traditional Color				Black	Chocolate	Cinnamon	Blue	Lilac	Fawn	Red	Cream	White

Sepia & Mink Color	Seal	Chocolate	Cinnamon	Blue	Lilac	Fawn	Red	Cream

Head: modified wedge with flat planes.
Body: foreign.

Copper	Gold	Yellow	Hazel
Green	Aqua	Blue	Odd Eyes

To conform to coat color

Russian Blue Blue

Russian Blue Blue

and they could not believe this tiny, red, screaming baby would ever grow into a beautiful princess. So they gently placed their gifts in another crib from which only quiet purring emanated. And that is how the Russian Blue came to be such a beautiful and gifted cat!

Appearance

The body is long and graceful in outline, with a long tapering tail, long legs, and small, oval-shaped feet. The Russian Blue is a powerful, elegant cat with a long, well-muscled body and graceful carriage. It is not a cat of extremes—it is neither fine nor cobby—but it gives the impression of strength. It may look heavier than it actually is because of the plushness of the coat. Russian females have a slightly finer build, a smaller body, and a sweet, serene expression. The modified wedge-shaped head is made up of a series of flat planes, with a flat skull, broad at eye level, a nose of medium

length, and a strong chin. The ears are large, wide at the base, and set as much on the side of the head as on the top. Eyes are wide set, almost round in shape, and a vivid green in color.

The Australian Russian Blue is bred to standards that differ greatly from the Russian Blue bred in the United States. The Australian Russian Blues have a longer body type and a "puffy" muzzle, looking as though the cat is puffing out its cheeks.

The Russian Blues that I saw in Moscow, Russia, were of semi-foreign type. They had deep, breathtaking emerald green eyes.

Color and Pattern

The Russian Blue is shown in the traditional category, solid division, in the blue color only.

Of interest, breeders in other parts of the world are working toward developing other colors, including the black, white, and pointed colors.

Temperament

Sweet, gentle, and shy by nature, Russian Blues are easily startled and prefer delicate handling. While they make excellent, loving, playful companions to their owners, they can be cautious with strangers. Russian Blues seem to prefer the security of their family and home. They are perfectly content to remain indoors, sit by their favorite window, and watch the world go by. They are sensitive and affectionate, and they enjoy the company of their owners. Russian Blues do not need much space in order to feel comfortable. Highly intelligent, these cats are mechanically inclined and often very receptive to games and training—several are known to have "trained" their owners to throw toys for them to retrieve.

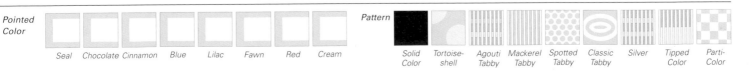

Pointed Color								Pattern								
Seal	Chocolate	Cinnamon	Blue	Lilac	Fawn	Red	Cream		Solid Color	Tortoise-shell	Agouti Tabby	Mackerel Tabby	Spotted Tabby	Classic Tabby	Silver	Tipped Color	Parti-Color

NEBELUNG

The Nebelung (which means "creature of the mist" in German) is a longhaired blue cat, with silver tipping, creating silver mist over the cat.

Nebelung Blue

Copper Gold Yellow Hazel

Green Aqua Blue Odd Eyes
Green only

Head: modified wedge with flat planes. Body: foreign.

Appearance

The head is a series of flat planes, with the large ears set far apart, as much on the sides of the head as on the top of the head. The green eyes are almost round but may appear to be oval at times. The body is foreign in type. The silver-tipped coat is medium-long, with a dense undercoat that causes the hair to stand out away from the body. Because the Russian Blue is the allowed outcross for providing genetic diversity in the Nebelung, some of the resulting kittens may have a shorter coat than required by the show standard.

Color and Pattern

The Nebelung is recognized in the blue color only, in the traditional category, solid division.

Temperament

The Nebelung is sweet and gentle by nature, highly intelligent, and loving to its owners and family members; it may, however, be shy with strangers, especially young children. Kittens may need time to adjust to their new home. If they are allowed to adjust at their own pace, they should become devoted companions. Once Nebelungs have bonded with their owner, they become quite affectionate and will follow their owner from room to room. If allowed, these cats enjoy sleeping on their owner's bed. This is a nice, quiet, reserved, undemanding breed, very nicely suited for apartment living.

General Description

The Nebelung is a semi-longhaired cat of foreign type; the texture of the coat is silky. The Nebelung is the only long-haired breed that comes solely in the blue color. The long, silver-tipped hair and intense green eyes dazzle the eye of the viewer.

History

From its ancient, mystical beginnings in Northern Russia, the Nebelung is making a comeback in modern society. With its long silky hair and elegant body, the Nebelung breeders wish to recreate the Russian Blue longhair. This gorgeous cat was exhibited in the very first British cat shows more than one hundred years ago. Today the Nebelung is recognized as a championship breed in TICA.

This cat's modern renaissance began in 1986, at Nebelheim ("Home of the Mist" in German) cattery located in the Denver, Colorado, area. Siegfried (born in 1984) and Brunhilde (born in 1985) were the first registered Nebelungs. They produced their first litter in 1986. Shortly thereafter, the Nebelung was accepted as a new breed in TICA, and in 1997 it was accepted for champion status. The breed is also accepted in champion-ship status in several other cat fanciers organizations.

Traditional Color	Black	Chocolate	Cinnamon	Blue	Lilac	Fawn	Red	Cream	White	Sepia & Mink Color	Seal	Chocolate	Cinnamon	Blue	Lilac	Fawn	Red	Cream

New Russian Colors

The Russian Blue in North America is shown only in solid blue color. However, breeders in other countries are working on other colors. The colors are, at the present moment, Black Russians, White Russians, and Pointed Russians. Regardless of the color or pattern, these cats should conform to the Russian Blue Standard.

The head should be a modified wedge with all seven flat planes. These planes are as follows: a straight line from the top of the head to the eye brow; a straight line from the eye brow to the tip of the nose; a straight line from the tip of the nose to the bottom of the chin; a straight line from the base of the ears to the muzzle; a straight line from the beginning of the muzzle to the end of the muzzle. (In Australia, a puffy muzzle is preferred.) The ears are large and set low on the sides of the head. The ears may appear to be smaller due to their low set. The eyes are a large oval in shape.

The cats should have a foreign body type and a double coat. By foreign type, it is meant that the body should be long, the legs should be long and slim. Distinctive also is the neck, which is arched. The neck and the head resemble a cobra. The body may appear heavier than it actually is, due to the thickness of the coat.

The hair color of the Blacks, Whites, and Pointeds will not be tipped in "silver" as in the Blue Russians. Also the chances are that these new colors may not have the density of coat.

We have known that the Pointed Gene is in the Russian Blue gene pool for some time, as the Russian Blues have been know to have pointed kittens. In this gene pool, there could also be the *ca* gene that could result in a white cat with pale blue eyes. If the breeders are working with the Dominant White Gene, then any eye color would be possible, as the Dominant White Gene is a masking gene. This would mean that if two White Russians, each of which were heterozygous (*W/w x W/w*), were bred together, the kittens could be any color or pattern that the parents had in the genotype.

A Russian is distinguished by its type (mentioned above) and not by its color. One should be able to color a Russian with any color and still be able to determine it is a Russian.

139

Pointed Russian Blue Point

Russian Black Black

Pointed Color   Seal   Chocolate   Cinnamon   Blue   Lilac   Fawn   Red   Cream

Pattern   Solid Color   Tortoiseshell   Agouti Tabby   Mackerel Tabby   Spotted Tabby   Classic Tabby   Silver   Tipped Color   Parti-Color

Scottish Fold/Scottish Fold Longhair

With its folded-down ears and huge eyes, the Scottish Fold resembles an owl.

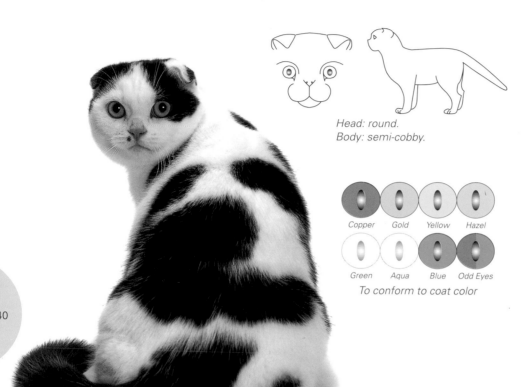

Head: round.
Body: semi-cobby.

Copper | Gold | Yellow | Hazel

Green | Aqua | Blue | Odd Eyes

To conform to coat color

General Description

The Scottish Fold is a blend of the American and British Shorthairs, leaning toward the British in appearance. Its British Shorthair heritage gives it a rounded head and a nice, chunky, semi-cobby body. The Scottish Folds come in both shorthair and longhair varieties.

History

In 1961, a white kitten with folded-down ears was born on the McRae farm in the Tayside region of Scotland. William Ross, a shepherd who lived next door, noticed the cat, which was later to be named Susie. The McRaes promised to alert Ross and his wife, Mary, a cat lover, if any more kittens with folded ears appeared. Two years later Susie had kittens, and two in the litter had folded ears. One of these, a

Scottish Fold Black Smoke & White

Scottish Fold Brown Mackerel Tabby

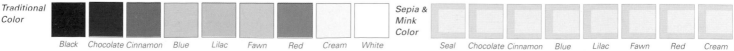

Traditional Color									Sepia & Mink Color							
Black	Chocolate	Cinnamon	Blue	Lilac	Fawn	Red	Cream	White		Seal	Chocolate	Cinnamon	Blue	Lilac	Fawn	Red	Cream

Scottish Fold White

Scottish Fold Brown Classic Tabby & White

white female named Snooks, was given to the Rosses. They bred Snooks to a red tabby domestic cat, thus producing a white male with folded ears they called Snowball. They then acquired a white British Shorthair, named Lady May, and started their breeding program for Scottish Folds.

Appearance

The Scottish Fold is of medium size, never massive or cobby; it is semi-cobby in type. The head is rather broad (but not as broad as that of an Exotic Shorthair or Persian). There is a slight stop between the eye ridge and the beginning of the nose. The muzzle is rather short (again, not like the Exotic Shorthair or Persian) and is a little longer than that of the British Shorthair. The large, round eyes are spaced well apart; the cat will look straight into your eyes with a sweet and loving gaze. The coat is dense whether the hair is short or long, adding to the overall appearance of a soft, cuddly teddy bear.

All Scottish Fold kittens are born with straight ears. Because the folding of the ears is the result of a dominant gene, not all kittens in a Scottish Fold litter will have folded ears. Between the ages of thirteen and twenty-three days old, a crimp will develop in the pinna of the ears of the kittens that will have folded ears.

Some breeders have different opinions as to inherited genetic problems connected with this breed. While some claim a Scottish Fold may be bred to another Scottish Fold with no trouble, others claim that serious defects may show up when the cat reaches the age of five years or older. The gene that causes the ear to fold may also affect the cartilage in other parts of the cat's body. Abnormalities such as gnarling of the feet, an arthritis-like condition, or cartilage growth around the joints (causing difficulty in walking) may occur. If serious problems are to appear later on, the kitten's tail will often be stiff, not flexible, almost hard to the touch, and it may make a snapping sound when it is handled.

Color and Pattern

All colors of all divisions of the traditional and pointed categories are accepted.

The density of the Scottish Fold's fur gives the coat the look of a thick rug adorned with intense colors.

Temperament

Scottish Folds are hardy cats (other than the difficulty mentioned above). Their sweet disposition matches their sweet expression. They have tiny voices and are not exceptionally vocal. They adore human companionship and have a gentle way about them that endears them to their human companions. Due to their easy nature, Scottish Folds readily adapt to almost any home situation. They do not mind noisy children or other animals. They also adapt nicely to apartment life.

Pointed Color

Seal Chocolate Cinnamon Blue Lilac Fawn Red Cream

Pattern

Solid Color Tortoise-shell Agouti Tabby Mackerel Tabby Spotted Tabby Classic Tabby Silver Tipped Color Parti Color

SCOTTISH FOLD LONGHAIR

As the name suggests, this cat is the longhair version of the Scottish Fold.

General Description

Relatively rare, the longhair version of the Scottish Fold is like the shorthair in type; the two cats differ only in coat length and texture. The semi-longhaired coat is quite thick.

History

In England, the British Shorthair had often been used as an outcross for this breed, and the Persian had been used as an outcross for the British; the longhair gene was bound to surface. The Scottish Fold Longhair was accepted in TICA for championship status in February 1987.

Why do we not see more Scottish Fold Longhairs? There are two genes involved. When a heterozygous breeding takes place, the resulting litter could be made up of kittens with straight ears only, kittens with straight or folded ears, or, if the breeder is lucky, kittens with folded ears only. The other gene is for long hair, which is recessive to the gene for short hair.

The breeders are faced with trying to breed two Scottish Fold Longhairs or two Scottish Fold Shorthairs, each carrying the gene for longhair; or to breed a Scottish Fold Longhair to a Scottish Fold Shorthair in hopes that the Shorthair is carrying the longhair gene. These breedings are not recommended, because there is a risk that the kittens could grow up to be crippled adults. As in the Scottish Fold Shorthair, the gene causing the ears to "fold" is a mutation, resulting in a dominant gene. This gene affects the cartilage in the ear, causing it to fold back. This gene may affect the cartilage in other parts of the cat's body when the cat is five or more years of age, and could cause it to be crippled. It is best to breed a Scottish Fold to a straight-eared cat. It is also advisable, when buying a Scottish Fold kitten, to make sure that one parent was a straight-eared cat. Not all Scottish Folds have the tendency to become crippled. Some Scottish Folds have been reported to live past ten years of age in perfect health. Breeders are generally very careful in their breeding of these cats and avoid using any Scottish Fold that exhibits an early sign of crippling or any cat that has produced kittens that later became crippled.

Scottish Fold Longhair Silver Mackerel Torbie

Traditional Color	Black	Chocolate	Cinnamon	Blue	Lilac	Fawn	Red	Cream	White	Sepia & Mink Color	Seal	Chocolate	Cinnamon	Blue	Lilac	Fawn	Red	Cream

Head: round. Body: semi-cobby.

Copper   Gold   Yellow   Hazel

Green   Aqua   Blue   Odd Eyes

To conform to coat color

Scottish Fold Longhair Brown Mackerel Torbie & White

Appearance

The coat of the shorthaired Scottish Fold is nice and thick, but the coat of the Scottish Fold Longhair is luxurious to the touch, especially if the British Shorthair was used for outcrossing. Due to the long hair, the ears are almost hidden from view. Like the shorthaired version, it is possible to put a hand on top of this cat's head and not touch the tips of the ears. Running one's fingers through this soft, silky, long coat is a true pleasure.

Color and Pattern

All colors of all divisions of the traditional and pointed categories are accepted.

Temperament

If the Scottish Fold Shorthair is an easygoing breed, then the Scottish Fold Longhair is a positively go-with-the-flow, carefree breed. These cats make wonderful pets and companions for the people who appreciate the Scottish Fold Longhair's beauty and quiet, gentle outlook on life. They are not demanding cats and are content just to be with you.

Scottish Fold Longhair Red Classic Tabby & White

Pointed Color

Seal   Chocolate   Cinnamon   Blue   Lilac   Fawn   Red   Cream

Pattern

Solid Color   Tortoise-shell   Agouti Tabby   Mackerel Tabby   Spotted Tabby   Classic Tabby   Silver   Tipped Color   Parti-Color

Selkirk Rex

The curly coat of the Selkirk Rex gives it the appearance of a cat in sheep's clothing.

Selkirk Rex Red Mackerel Tabby

General Description

The Selkirk Rex, one of the newer recognized breeds, is distinguished by a coat made up of curls. The Selkirk Rex comes in both the short- and longhaired varieties, and its curls are, of course, more pronounced in the longhaired version. This cat has a semi-cobby body, a pleasantly round head, round eyes, and medium-sized ears. Its body type is is similar to that of the British Shorthair, one of the accepted outcrosses for the Selkirk Rex.

History

A blue tortie and white shorthaired female cat, later named Miss DePesto (born in 1987), was found in a Wyoming shelter. She was given to a Montana Persian breeder, who bred her to a black Persian. This breeding produced six kittens, three of which had curly coats. After further breedings, it became clear that the curly-hair gene was dominant. When the standard for the breed was being determined, it was decided that all

Head: round.
Body: semi-cobby.

Copper Gold Yellow Hazel

Green Aqua Blue Odd Eyes

No relationship between eye color and coat color.

Traditional Color									Sepia & Mink Color							
Black	Chocolate	Cinnamon	Blue	Lilac	Fawn	Red	Cream	White	Seal	Chocolate	Cinnamon	Blue	Lilac	Fawn	Red	Cream

Selkirk Rex Seal Point

Selkirk Rex Tortie Point

145

Selkirk Rex Cream Mackerel Tabby

Selkirk Rex Longhair Black

Pointed
Color

Seal Chocolate Cinnamon Blue Lilac Fawn Red Cream

Pattern

Solid
Color Tortoise-
shell Agouti
Tabby Mackerel
Tabby Spotted
Tabby Classic
Tabby Silver Tipped
Color Parti-
Color

Selkirk Rex Seal Tortie Point & White

Selkirk Rex Longhair White

colors and both hair lengths were allowed, since Miss DePesto carried both the pointed and the longhair genes.

Appearance

The Selkirk Rex is a semi-cobby breed of cat, with sturdy bone structure and strong muscles. The head is round, the eyes are round, and the muzzle is round. The nose is short (but not as short as the nose of a Persian); there is a stop below the eyebrows at the beginning of the nose.

In a new litter of kittens, it is easy to tell which ones will have curly hair. They are the ones born with curly whiskers.

As these kittens get older, the ends of these curly whiskers become brittle and break off, leaving very short, curly whiskers. At approximately four months, the kittens go through an awkward stage when many lose most of their hair. When their hair grows back, the hair is once again curled, and it remains that way from then on.

The shorthaired coat is thick and of medium length. The hairs are arranged in loose individual curls, which are particularly prominent in the neck and tail areas. The guard hairs are slightly coarse, but the overall effect is still one of softness and plushness. The longhair has soft, dense, semi-long hair with loose, individual curls.

These curls give the breed a distinctive, shaggy appearance and make the coat pleasant to the touch.

Color and Pattern

The Selkirk Rex is recognized in all categories, all divisions, and all colors.

When the white spotting is present, the pattern takes on a look that is different from the straighthaired breeds, due to the clustering of the individual curls. This is especially true in the Selkirk Rex Longhair, because the curls are longer and fuller.

Temperament

The Selkirk Rex are very sweet and loyal. They are a healthy breed and make gentle, pleasant companions.

above: Selkirk Rex Longhair White.
below: Selkirk Rex Red & White

The Siamese are the svelte ballet dancers of the cat world.

| Copper | Gold | Yellow | Hazel |
| Green | Aqua | Blue | Odd Eyes |

To conform to coat color

Siamese Lynx Point

Traditional Color									Sepia & Mink Color							
Black	Chocolate	Cinnamon	Blue	Lilac	Fawn	Red	Cream	White	Seal	Chocolate	Cinnamon	Blue	Lilac	Fawn	Red	Cream

Head: wedge, straight lines.
Body: Oriental.

Siamese Chocolate Point

Siamese Seal Point

General Description

The Siamese is a sleek, elegant cat that glides on its tall, slender legs. The Oriental type, which is shared by the Siamese, Balinese, Oriental Shorthair, and Oriental Longhair, is characterized by large ears, a wedge-shaped head, a long neck, a long tubular body, long slim legs, and a long, whippy, pointed tail.

History

One of the oldest known breeds of domestic cat, the Siamese is reported to have originated in Siam (now Thailand). The Siamese, as evidenced by art and literature over the centuries, were cared for and protected within Siam's temple walls and royal palaces as far back as the fourteenth century. These cats, which displayed a wide range of coat colors and patterns, were offered as gifts to special guests of the royal family of Siam. The Siamese cat was introduced to the western world in the early 1800s, undoubtedly when one of these treasured cats was presented to a European dignitary.

Seal point Siamese began appearing in English cat shows in the late nineteenth century and in North America in the early twentieth century. Despite the range of colors and patterns shown on the original Siamese, cat shows of the early twentieth century limited the Siamese coat to the pointed pattern. Around 1934, Siamese with the blue point color were shown and recognized, followed by those with the chocolate point, and, in 1955, the lilac point. The early Siamese in England and North America were not as extreme as the Siamese of today, in that the head was a shorter wedge and the eyes were either oval or round, and the body was semi-cobby to semi-foreign in shape. This type of Siamese is still loved and promoted by the Traditional Siamese organization; not everyone likes the extreme look of the modern show Siamese.

Appearance

The Siamese is famed for its sleek beauty—a stunning contrast of dark point color, lighter body color, and the most extraordinary blue eyes. Oriental in type, the Siamese should have a tubular torso, resting on long, fine-boned legs, and ending with a long, whippy tail that seems to go on forever. The wedge is created by straight lines extending from the nose to the tips of the ears, forming a triangle, with no break at the whiskers. The desirable profile may be seen as a long flat, straight line extending from the top of the head to the tip of the nose, or as two flat planes with a very slight change in angle midway over the eyes. The nose must be straight, without a hint of a dip or rise. The large, broad-based ears flare outward and are angled slightly forward, completing the triangular head as a continuation of the wedge. The ears must not sit on top of the head like those of a donkey, as this type of ear set would not be a continuation of the wedge-shaped head. The medium-sized, almond-shaped eyes

149

Pointed Color								Pattern							
Seal	Chocolate	Cinnamon	Blue	Lilac	Fawn	Red	Cream	Solid Color	Tortoise-shell	Agouti Tabby	Tabby (Lynx)	Spotted Tabby	Classic Tabby	Silver	Tipped Color	Parti-Color

Siamese Red Point

Siamese Seal Point

Siamese Blue Point

should be approximately one eye's width apart, with the inner aperture slanting toward the nose and the outer aperture in line with the center of the ear base. Crossed eyes are considered a penalty. These cats must feel as hard as a rock; there must be nothing flabby, mushy, or soft about them.

Color and Pattern

The Siamese is recognized in the pointed category, in all divisions, in all pointed colors, including seal point, chocolate point, lilac point, blue point, cinnamon point, fawn point, red point, and cream point.

It includes all pointed colors of the solid points, tortie points, lynx points, silver lynx points, shaded or chinchilla points, smoke points, and parti-color points.

The eyes are a brilliant sapphire blue.

Temperament

The Siamese, Balinese, Oriental Shorthair, and Oriental Longhair are vocal to the point of loudness, and are quite active. Nothing gives them more pleasure than to sit in their owner's lap, sleep in their owner's bed, and even share their owner's pillow. They want to be as close as possible, and their need for closeness verges on the desperate. These cats are intelligent, inquisitive, even nosy—they will investigate and comment on everything their owner does. Indeed, these are demanding cats. However, to please a Siamese is simply to hold it, stroke it, talk to it, and love it. To please a Siamese is to have a friend for life.

Siamese Lilac Point

left: Siamese Seal Point. center: Siamese Blue Point. right: Siamese Blue Point.

BALINESE

The Balinese is a longhaired Siamese—a ballerina in flowing skirts.

Copper	Gold	Yellow	Hazel
Green	Aqua	Blue	Odd Eyes

To conform to coat color

Balinese Lilac Point

Balinese Blue Point

General Description

The Balinese is a pointed, semi-longhaired Siamese. With their semi-longhaired coat, points, wedge-shaped head, tubular body, and blue eyes, the Balinese seen in exhibitions today are indeed breathtaking.

History

Early Balinese cats were reported to be the product of Siamese-to-Siamese breeding. It has been stated that a longhaired Siamese was registered with C.F.F. (Cat Fancier's Federation) in 1928. CFF is a cat registering organization located in Ohio. It is likely that the longhair gene was introduced into the Siamese gene pool in England during the World Wars, when breeders needed to outcross in order to retain a part of the cats' bloodlines. Longhaired Siamese were recognized in 1961 as a separate breed and given the name Balinese because these cats were reminiscent of Balinese temple dancers. CFA recognized the cat in 1970 and called it the Javanese. When TICA was formed in 1979, the Balinese came as an established championship breed.

Appearance

Like the Siamese, the Balinese is a series of narrow triangles and tubes; it also is Oriental in type. The standards of the Balinese and the Siamese are almost identical, except for the length of the coat.

The semi-longhaired coat is to be fine and silky, lying close to the body. The coat may be shorter around the head and shoulders. The length of the slender tail should be balanced with the length of the body; the tail plume should be long and feathery. Because of its longer coat, the Balinese will appear to have softer lines and a less extreme type than the Oriental Shorthair or Siamese. However, when the coat is smoothed down the underlying bone structure can be discerned.

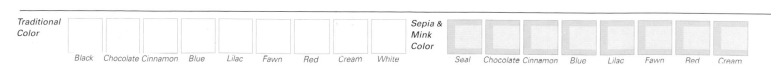

Traditional Color										Sepia & Mink Color							
	Black	Chocolate	Cinnamon	Blue	Lilac	Fawn	Red	Cream	White		Seal	Chocolate	Cinnamon	Blue	Lilac	Fawn	Red	Cream

Balinese Red Point

Balinese Seal Lynx Point

Color and Pattern

The Balinese is shown only in the pointed category, in all divisions. All pointed colors of the solid points, tortie points, lynx points, silver lynx points, shaded points, chinchilla points, smoke points, and particolor points are included.

Although a range of color within each color class is permitted, there should be a definite contrast between the body and the points. A lack of leg and tail barring, or tabby stripe marking, is desirable, except in lynx points; a lack of body barring is desirable in all patterns.

Temperament

Balinese make sweet, loving pets.

Head: wedge, straight lines.
Body: Oriental.

Pointed Color								Pattern							
Seal	Chocolate	Cinnamon	Blue	Lilac	Fawn	Red	Cream	Solid Color	Tortoise-shell	Agouti Tabby	Tabby (Lynx)	Spotted Tabby	Classic Tabby	Silver	Tipped Color	Parti-Color

ORIENTAL SHORTHAIR

The Oriental is a Siamese with a "lacquered" coat in glorious colors and patterns.

General Description

This is a man-made breed, developed in the mid-twentieth century in an attempt to create a Siamese in a range of colors. Early efforts included outcrosses to other breeds, such as the Russian Blue, in order to bring in new colors and patterns. Although breeders tried to use cats that would most closely resemble the Siamese in type, the early Oriental Shorthair lost the type of the Siamese. It took time and effort for dedicated breeders to produce the beautiful Oriental Shorthairs that we see today.

History

The Siamese, in their ancestral home of Siam, displayed a range of colors (brown, black, shaded silver, white, and bicolored). In the 1920s only the pointed Siamese were recognized by the governing powers in England.

Therefore, the full-colored Siamese gradually disappeared from the gene pool.

The idea to create a breed like the Siamese, but with new colors and patterns, originated in England around 1950. Pat Turner (a well-known Siamese breeder and cat judge known and respected for her knowledge of feline genetics) worked with this early breed and was known for developing the Foreign Whites, as they were called.

In Britain the breeds were recognized by their color. In GCCF each color was given a unique name reflecting the color or pattern. The following colors were granted championship status:1958: Chestnut Brown Foreign championship status. 1970: the Chestnut Brown Foreign was renamed Havana, to reflect what the breeders wanted. 1977: Foreign Lilac and the Foreign White. 1980: Oriental Black

Oriental Shorthair Chocolate Tortie & White

Copper   Gold   Yellow   Hazel

Green   Aqua   Blue   Odd Eyes

Green preferred, gold accepted

Head: wedge, straight lines.
Body: Oriental.

Traditional Color	Black	Chocolate	Cinnamon	Blue	Lilac	Fawn	Red	Cream	White	Sepia & Mink Color	Seal	Chocolate	Cinnamon	Blue	Lilac	Fawn	Red	Cream

Oriental Shorthair Cinnamon Spotted Tabby

Oriental Shorthair Seal Classic Tabby

and Oriental Spotted Tabby. 1985: Oriental Blue and Oriental Red. 1989: Oriental Tortie. 1996: Oriental Cinnamon and Oriental Shaded. 1999: Oriental Cream and Oriental Fawn.

It should be noted that other colors and patterns are being added to the GCCF registry. In TICA the Oriental Shorthair is recognized not by individual colors or patterns, but as a collective breed to include all colors of the Traditional Category.

In the 1980s, TICA allowed the pointed offspring from an Oriental Shorthair breeding to be shown with the Siamese and registered as an Oriental Shorthair variant.

Appearance

The elegant Oriental Shorthair is identical in type to the Siamese. Its short, close-lying coat comes in a range of colors and looks as if it has been painted on with a high-gloss lacquer.

Color and Pattern

The Oriental Shorthair is accepted in all colors and all divisions, in the traditional category.

The basic colors are black, chocolate, cinnamon, and red. The dilutions are blue, lilac, fawn, and cream. Although white is not a color, it is also included.

Temperament

The Oriental Shorthair will not accept being ignored. These cats, like the others in this breed group, may be called "under-your-feet" cats. They will cuddle and snuggle up to you. Their desire to be near you is so sweet and loving that it cannot be denied.

Pointed Color

Seal	Chocolate	Cinnamon	Blue	Lilac	Fawn	Red	Cream

Pattern

Solid Color	Tortoise-shell	Agouti Tabby	Mackerel Tabby	Spotted Tabby	Classic Tabby	Silver	Tipped Color	Parti-Color

Oriental Shorthair Silver Classic Tabby

Oriental Shorthair Blue

Oriental Shorthair White

Oriental Shorthair Chocolate Spotted Tabby

Oriental Shorthair Silver Classic Tabby

Oriental Longhair

The Oriental Longhair is a Siamese with a semi-longhaired coat in glorious colors and patterns.

General Description

A refined cat of medium size, the Oriental Longhair shares the standard for the Oriental Shorthair, the only difference being its semi-longhaired coat.

History

The first registered U.S.-born Oriental Longhair litter arrived in 1985, thus starting the breed in this country. TICA was the first American association to recognize the Oriental Longhair for championship status, and in 1995 CFA accepted the Oriental Longhair in a division within the Oriental Shorthair. In England, Oriental Longhairs are known as Angoras. In parts of Europe, Oriental Longhairs are known as Javanese.

Oriental Longhair Brown Mackerel Tabby

Copper   Gold   Yellow   Hazel

Green   Aqua   Blue   Odd Eyes

Green preferred,
gold accepted

Oriental Longhair Black

Head: wedge, straight lines.
Body: Oriental.

Oriental Longhair Blue

Traditional Color	Black	Chocolate	Cinnamon	Blue	Lilac	Fawn	Red	Cream	White	Sepia & Mink Color	Seal	Chocolate	Cinnamon	Blue	Lilac	Fawn	Red	Cream

Oriental Longhair White

The Oriental Longhair is relatively rare. It is very difficult for breeders to keep the type and the semi-longhaired coat at the same time. The breeders must go back to the Oriental Shorthair or the Siamese in order to keep the type of these breeds; in doing so, they may lose coat length. It takes years of breeding in order to establish both type and the semi-longhaired coat.

Appearance

With the exception of its coat length, the Oriental Longhair is identical to the Oriental Shorthair. This is a full-colored, longhaired version of the Oriental Shorthair that is identical in type to the Siamese. Balance and proportion are considered to be of great consequence in this breed.

Color and Pattern

The Oriental Longhair is recognized in all colors, all divisions, in the traditional category.

The basic colors are black, chocolate, cinnamon, and red. The dilutions are blue, lilac, fawn, and cream. Although white is not a color, it is included.

Temperament

The Oriental Longhair is somewhat more sedate than its cousin, the Oriental Shorthair, but not much. Like its relatives, the Siamese, Balinese, and Oriental Shorthair, it is an active, demanding, "under-your-feet" kind of cat.

Pointed Color

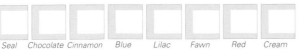

Seal *Chocolate* *Cinnamon* *Blue* *Lilac* *Fawn* *Red* *Cream*

Pattern

Solid Color *Tortoise-shell* *Agouti Tabby* *Mackerel Tabby* *Spotted Tabby* *Classic Tabby* *Silver* *Tipped Color* *Parti-Color*

Siberian

The defender of the household, the thick-coated Siberian is a large, stately cat that originated in Russia.

Siberian Brown Mackerel Tabby & White

General Description

The Siberian is a large, strong, thick-coated cat. Its appearance tells of great strength, power, and size, excellent physical condition, and alertness; yet its facial expression is quite sweet. Despite its size, this cat is extremely agile and adept at leaping due to its mighty muscles and build. The back is long and very slightly arched when the cat is still, but it looks horizontal when in motion. The waist is muscular and convex in shape, and the round, compact belly develops with age. The hind legs, when straightened, are slightly longer than the forelegs. The paws are round, big, and quite powerful. This cat is made up of roundness and circular shapes (although the head will still "fit" into a modified wedge), as opposed to the rectangles and triangles that are seen in similar breeds.

History

The Siberian, native to Russia, is an ancient breed that originated perhaps a thousand years ago. It is said that these exceptionally strong, agile cats resided in Russian monasteries and acted as guards, watching for intruders from their perches atop high beams. The Russian monks cared for and treated them as beloved pets. The first Siberians to be imported to the United States arrived on June 28, 1990, to be owned by breeder Elizabeth Terrell (Starpoint Cattery) of Baton Rouge, LA. The Siberian may be the ancestor of the Norwegian Forest Cat and of the Maine Coon.

Appearance

The head is a modified wedge of medium size with rounded contours, broader at the skull and narrowing slightly to a full, rounded muzzle (shorter than that of a Maine Coon or Norwegian Forest Cat), with a well-rounded chin. In Russia, the trapezoid-shaped head, broad at the top and narrowing slightly toward the bottom, with a broad, blunt muzzle is preferred. This combination gives a sweet expression to the face. The top of the head is flat, with a gentle slope from the forehead to the nose and a slight concave curve before the tip of the nose. The transition between the muzzle and the side of the head is subtle. The cheekbones are

Siberian Brown Mackerel Tabby

Traditional Color	Black	Chocolate	Cinnamon	Blue	Lilac	Fawn	Red	Cream	White	Sepia & Mink Color	Seal	Chocolate	Cinnamon	Blue	Lilac	Fawn	Red	Cream

Head: modified wedge with rounded contours.
Body: large, substantial, moderately long.

| Copper | Gold | Yellow | Hazel |
| Green | Aqua | Blue | Odd Eyes |

No relationship to coat color

Siberian Blue Mackerel Tabby

neither high-set nor prominent. There should be a good distance between the ears and eyes. The large, almost round eyes are set wide with the outer corner angled slightly up. The ears are medium-large, wide, and set on the corners of the head, with rounded, forward-tilting tips. Lynx tipping is desirable. The well-muscled neck is medium-long, rounded, and substantial.

The Siberian's long, thick coat is similar to that of the Norwegian Forest Cat, with a tight undercoat that thickens in cold weather. The Russians refer to this coat as being "triple coated"

with all hairs being of equal length. An abundant ruff sets off the cat's large, impressive head; hair on the shoulder blades and lower part of the chest is slightly shorter. The hair may thicken to curls on the belly and breeches (britches).

Color and Pattern

The Siberian is shown in the traditional category, in all colors of all divisions.

Temperament

The Siberian is a strong, independent cat that needs plenty of living space in

which to roam. It is not a lap cat, but will have a very special bonding with the people it loves. Siberians are said to have a devotion to their loved owners that is "dog-like."

Siberian Blue Mackerel Tabby & White

COMPARING THE MAINE COON, NORWEGIAN FOREST CAT, AND THE SIBERIAN

	Maine Coon	Norwegian Forest Cat	Siberian
Head	Broad, Modified Wedge, High Prominent Cheekbones. Square muzzle. Profile: Slight slope.	Equilateral triangular, all straight lines from forehead to tip of nose; muzzle fits into triangular shape.	Large, broad, modified wedge with rounded contours. Rounded muzzle. Profile: slight slope.
Body	Long, rectangular, substantial. Legs medium long; to fit into rectangle with body.	Medium in length, square in appearance. Legs medium long; hind legs longer.	Heavy, moderately long. Back slightly arched. Legs moderately long.
Coat	Uneven, falls smoothly. All-weather coat.	Double coat, full ruff, oily, water repellent	Triple coat, full ruff, oily, water resistant.

Pointed Color

| Seal | Chocolate | Cinnamon | Blue | Lilac | Fawn | Red | Cream |

Pattern

| Solid Color | Tortoise-shell | Agouti Tabby | Mackerel Tabby | Spotted Tabby | Classic Tabby | Silver | Tipped Color | Parti-Color |

Singapura

The Puma of the cat fancy dressed in oatmeal and cream.

General Description

The Singapura is a ticked tabby, with sable coloring. This cat is stunning in appearance. The base color is an antique ivory, pale and almost translucent. The sable (seal sepia) color provides a wonderful contrast with the ivory color bands on each hair shaft. The Singapura is a medium- to small-sized cat with eyes that are disproportionately large for its face.

History

The Singapura traces its ancestry to diminutive, ticked tabby cats that were picked up off the streets of Singapore and brought to the United States to be a part of a carefully controlled breeding program. Siamese breeder Mrs. Tommy Meadows, of the United States, noticed these cats when she was living in Singapore. She returned home with five of them and began breeding these cats. Singapuras, Abyssinians, and Burmese were used in her breeding program in order to achieve the look she wanted.

Appearance

The compact Singapura is a medium- to small-sized semi-cobby, muscular cat with a small, rounded head and large, striking eyes. The sable (seal sepia) ticked tabby coloring almost shimmers on the short coat.

The head should be rounded, with a medium-short muzzle. The end of the

162

| Copper | Gold | Yellow | Hazel |
| Green | Celadon Green | Blue | Odd Eyes |

No relationship to coat color

Singapura Sable Ticked Tabby

Traditional Color									Sepia & Mink Color							
Black	Chocolate	Cinnamon	Blue	Lilac	Fawn	Red	Cream	White	Seal	Chocolate	Cinnamon	Blue	Lilac	Fawn	Red	Cream

Head: round.
Body: semi-cobby.

Singapura Sable Ticked Tabby

Singapura Sable Ticked Tabby

Singapura Sable Ticked Tabby

muzzle should be blunt. The alert-looking ears should be large and of medium distance from each other. The large, almond-shaped eyes are accented by "eyeliner" and encircled by a light-colored area.

Color and Pattern

The Singapura is recognized in the sepia category, tabby division, in the sable (seal sepia) ticked color only.

The coloring consists of alternating bands of dark seal brown ticking on a warm, antique ivory ground color. Muzzle, chin, chest, and stomach are the color of unbleached muslin. Nose leather is pale to dark salmon. The "eyeliner," nose outline, lips, whisker apertures, and hair between the toes are sable brown. The head must be ticked. There must be barring on the inner front legs and on the back of the knees. Well-defined facial markings should set off the eyes in contrast to the lighter base color. Curved "puma markings" should extend from the inside eye corners onto the cheeks. A definite tabby "M" is the only forehead pattern that is allowed.

Temperament

Known for their gentleness and soft voices, Singapuras are outgoing, even-tempered, affectionate cats. They adore human company. These alert, healthy animals can move at the speed of lightning when something catches their interest; they love to climb and enjoy viewing their surroundings from elevated perches. Since they are not terribly interested in the outdoors, they are well suited to apartment life.

Pointed Color								*Pattern*								
Seal	Chocolate	Cinnamon	Blue	Lilac	Fawn	Red	Cream		Solid Color	Tortoise-shell	Agouti Tabby	Mackerel Tabby	Spotted Tabby	Classic Tabby	Silver	Tipped Color	Parti-Color

Snowshoe

The Snowshoe is a blue-eyed pointed beauty with white "snowshoe" feet.

Snowshoe Blue Point & White

General Description

The Snowshoe, created by breeding a Siamese to a bicolor American Shorthair, is a medium-sized cat that combines some of the heftiness of its American Shorthair ancestors with the length and suppleness of its Oriental ancestors. It is a well-balanced cat, neither too small nor too large; it is firm, muscular without being bulky, and deceptively powerful and agile. A long cat, it has the appearance of a runner rather than that of a weight-lifter.

History

The Snowshoe is the result of breeding a Siamese with a cat having the white spotting factor. The Snowshoe originated in 1960 when Dorothy Hinds Daugherty, of Kensing Cattery, Philadelphia, Pennsylvania, found three kittens in a litter of Siamese, each with four white feet. She liked the contrast between the point color and the stark white of the feet so much that she bred her Siamese with a bicolor American Shorthair. Continued breeding eventually produced the popular inverted "V" pattern (bicolor) of the current Snowshoe, as well as the mitted variety.

The Snowshoe was first recognized as an experimental breed. In subsequent years, as interest in the breed grew, the Snowshoe was given championship status by other cat associations, including two in North America. TICA recog-

nized the Snowshoe for Championship status in 1994.

Appearance

The semi-foreign-type body is muscular but should never appear cobby. Males are medium to medium-large in size; females are small to medium. The tail length is equal to the distance from the base of the tail to the shoulders. The long legs are muscular and firm, with back legs straight. Paws are round in appearance with oval tips. The head is a modified triangle, nearly equilateral in shape. The nose may appear to be considerably longer than it actually is due to variations

of the inverted "V" pattern. Older males may have a more rounded appearance due to stud jowls. The eyes are medium in size and oval in shape.

Snowshoe Blue Point & White

Traditional Color									Sepia & Mink Color							
Black	Chocolate	Cinnamon	Blue	Lilac	Fawn	Red	Cream	White	Seal	Chocolate	Cinnamon	Blue	Lilac	Fawn	Red	Cream

Snowshoe Seal Point & White

Color and Pattern

The Snowshoe is recognized in the pointed category, particolor division, solid point eumelanistic colors, mitted and bicolor patterns only.

In the mitted pattern, the muzzle may be point color only or any facial pattern, but you do not want a full or partial inverted "V". The bicolor pattern has the full or partial inverted "V". In both patterns, the white on the front legs should extend to the mid-leg and on the back legs to the mid-thigh area.

The point colors create a mask over the face, except in the white areas near the ears. Facial white may extend downward from the chin in a white bib. The ears should be covered entirely by point colors, with no white. The body color is a lighter shade than that of the points; shading may darken as the cat ages.

Temperament

The Snowshoe, which has inherited a certain Siamese-like aloofness, is a gentle, friendly, intelligent cat. It speaks in a soft, melodic voice. This cat is inquisitive, entertaining, and somewhat active and offers a lifetime of affectionate companionship to its owners. The Snowshoe fits comfortably in a multiple-cat household.

Snowshoe Seal Point & White

Copper	Gold	Yellow	Hazel
Green	Aqua	Blue	Odd Eyes

Blue only

Head: modified wedge
Body: semi-foreign

Pointed Color								Pattern								
Seal	Chocolate	Cinnamon	Blue	Lilac	Fawn	Red	Cream	Solid Color	Tortoise-shell	Agouti Tabby	Mackerel Tabby	Spotted Tabby	Classic Tabby	Silver	Tipped Color	Parti-Color

Sphynx

The "hairless" wrinkled wonder of the cat world.

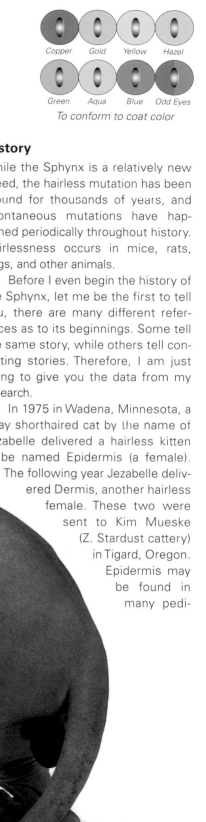

Copper Gold Yellow Hazel

Green Aqua Blue Odd Eyes

To conform to coat color

General Description

At first sight, the Sphynx causes extreme reactions. Some people are repulsed by it, and others are charmed. It is not a hairless cat; it is covered with a very short down that is almost invisible to the eye and undetectable to the touch; the points may have soft, short, dense hair, and a puff of hair may grace the tip of the tail. The wrinkled skin is highly susceptible to sunburn, so this cat should be kept indoors.

History

While the Sphynx is a relatively new breed, the hairless mutation has been around for thousands of years, and spontaneous mutations have happened periodically throughout history. Hairlessness occurs in mice, rats, dogs, and other animals.

Before I even begin the history of the Sphynx, let me be the first to tell you, there are many different references as to its beginnings. Some tell the same story, while others tell conflicting stories. Therefore, I am just going to give you the data from my research.

In 1975 in Wadena, Minnesota, a stray shorthaired cat by the name of Jezabelle delivered a hairless kitten to be named Epidermis (a female). The following year Jezabelle delivered Dermis, another hairless female. These two were sent to Kim Mueske (Z. Stardust cattery) in Tigard, Oregon. Epidermis may be found in many pedi-

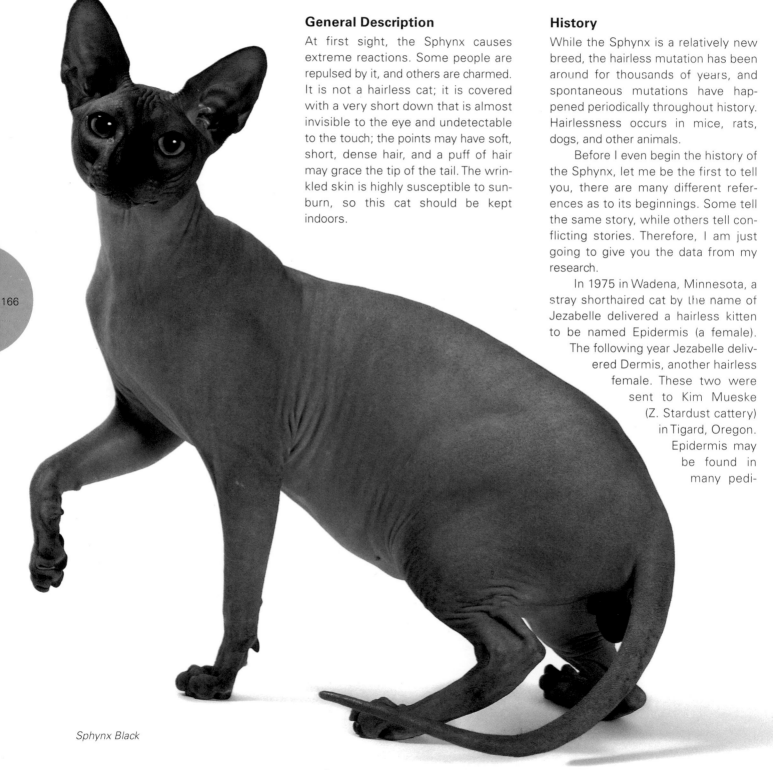

Sphynx Black

Traditional Color									Sepia & Mink Color							
Black	Chocolate	Cinnamon	Blue	Lilac	Fawn	Red	Cream	White	Seal	Chocolate	Cinnamon	Blue	Lilac	Fawn	Red	Cream

left: Sphynx Black & White.
right: Sphynx Chocolate Mink

Head: modified wedge with rounded contours.
Body: semi-foreign, medium with well rounded abdomen.

Sphynx Cream & White

Sphynx Red & White

grees and is considered to be an important influence on the Sphynx of today.

In 1966, in Toronto, Canada, a domestic cat, by the name of Elizabeth, produced a hairless kitten, named Prune.

In 1978, three hairless kittens were rescued from the streets of Toronto. These three cats may be the foundations for the Canadian (North American) Sphynx and maybe for some of the European Sphynx.

In 1980, Shirley Smith of Toronto obtained two hairless female kittens that were born from a domestic mother. Interestingly enough, it was reported they were sired by different fathers; if so each sire would have had to carry the recessive hairless gene. These kittens were named Punkie and Paloma. They were sent to the Netherlands.

Hairless cats have also shown up in Paris, France, and other parts of the world. Some of them were reported to be the offspring of Siamese, while other hairless kittens are from "stray" cats.

The Sphynx has been known as the "New Mexican Hairless," "Canadian Hairless," "Moon Cat," and "Chat sans Poil" (meaning the naked cat). In the 1970s it was given the name Sphynx.

The cat was given championship status in TICA in the 1980s. Since then, the Sphynx breed has captivated the cat world.

Appearance

The Sphynx is a medium-sized, muscular cat; it is not fine-boned or delicate. The wrinkled skin is covered with a fine down. There may be some short hair on the muzzle, feet, back of the ears, and tail. The head and torso should have good wrinkling. Kittens will have more wrinkles than the adults. The body features a broad chest, which tends toward the barrel shape. The abdomen should be well

Pointed Color								Pattern								
Seal	Chocolate	Cinnamon	Blue	Lilac	Fawn	Red	Cream		Solid Color	Tortoise-shell	Agouti Tabby	Mackerel Tabby	Spotted Tabby	Classic Tabby	Silver	Tipped Color	Parti-Color

Sphynx Black & White

rounded, as though the cat has eaten a large meal, but not so much that the cat is overweight. The toes are long, with thicker paw pads than those of other breeds. They can actually pick up objects with their long toes. The tail is long and tapered like a rat's tail. Due to the lack of hair, the Sphynx's body temperature seems to be about four degrees higher than that of other cats. It is for this reason the Sphynx is sometimes called a "hot water bottle cat." They need bathing more frequently than do cats with hair, in order to wash away the sweat secretions that accumulate in the wrinkles. The inside of the ears may need cleaning also, as there are no hairs to filter out dust.

The head of the Sphynx should be longer than it is wide, with gentle curves and prominent cheekbones. The muzzle should be strong and round, with a definite whisker break and a firm chin. The extremely large ears are set upright; they are neither low-set nor high-set. These cats have wrinkled foreheads and a characteristic worried look. The eyes should be a rounded lemon shape, slanting toward the outer ridge of the ear.

Color and Pattern

The Sphynx is shown in all colors of all divisions and in all categories.

Determining a Sphynx's color or pattern is a challenge. Since the skin is flesh colored, one must use the colors of the peach fuzz, the eyes, and the foot pads to find the answer. Blue eyes may mean the cat is pointed; mottled foot pads may indicate that the cat is a tortie or torbie.

Temperament

The Sphynx cat is highly active, vocal, and intelligent, with a passionate need to explore everything within reach. Characteristics of the Sphynx include infinite patience and willingness to put up with almost anything. They have been called "part monkey, part dog, part child, and part cat." They are indeed like monkeys in their level of activity, speed, and agility. These cats, especially the females in season, have loud voices; their "roar" puts the Siamese call to shame. However, the Sphynx cats are peaceful animals that make wonderful, sweet, loving pets.

Sphynx Blue Tortie & White

Sphynx Lilac Point & White.

Sphynx Brown Mackerel Tabby & White

Tonkinese

Once called the Golden Siamese, this is a charming short-haired cat in mink, sepia, and pointed solid colors, with a natural flowing body.

Tonkinese Chocolate (Champagne) Mink

General Description

The glamorous Tonkinese, famous for its "mink" coat, is moderate in size and type, a blend of Siamese and Burmese type and coloring. Nothing is extreme about this breed; its type, color, and disposition are moderate.

History

In the 1950s, a New York City cat owner named Milan Greer began breeding what he called "Golden Siamese," produced from breeding a Siamese to a Burmese, in an effort to produce cats with a rich mahogany body color and dark points. He began by crossing seal point Siamese to sable Burmese. By breeding together the offspring of the foundation cross, Greer claimed to have bred "pure" cats for five generations, producing only chocolate brown cats with seal or dark brown points. Greer's cats were enormously popular with pet buyers in New York City during the 1950s and early 1960s.

Tonkinese breeders trace their cats back to Wong Mau, a seal mink-colored cat, brought from Burma to the United States in the early 1930s. The breed was granted championship status by the Canadian Cat Association in 1971. Both CFA and TICA recognized the Tonkinese in 1979.

Appearance

The Tonkinese is a true blending of the Burmese and the Siamese, featuring the best attributes of both of these breeds. It is a medium-sized cat of semi-foreign type; the medium-short, modified-wedge-shaped head is softened by rounded contours. There is a stop between the eyebrow ridge and the beginning of the nose. Everything else should be medium, including the

Tonkinese Seal (Natural) Mink

Traditional Color									Sepia & Mink Color							
Black	Chocolate	Cinnamon	Blue	Lilac	Fawn	Red	Cream	White	Seal	Chocolate	Cinnamon	Blue	Lilac	Fawn	Red	Cream

Head: modified wedge with rounded contours. Body: semi-foreign.

Tonkinese Blue Mink

Tonkinese Lilac (Platinum) Mink

close-lying coat, which is medium-short, soft, fine, and silky. The coat requires little grooming to maintain its luxurious texture—a few sweeps with a rubber cat brush and an occasional bath are all that is required.

Color and Pattern

The Tonkinese are shown in the Sepia, Pointed, and Mink categories, eumelanistic colors only. These colors are: Seal Sepia, Seal Point, and Seal Mink; Chocolate Sepia, Chocolate Point, and Chocolate Mink; Cinnamon Sepia, Cinnamon Point, and Cinnamon Mink; Lilac Sepia, Lilac Point, and Lilac Mink; Blue Sepia, Blue Point, and Blue Mink; Fawn Sepia, Fawn Point, and Fawn Mink.

Temperament

Tonkinese are very adaptable, social creatures. They possess the intelligence of the Siamese and the affectionate nature of the Burmese—it might even be said that they received the affectionate natures of both breeds. Like the Siamese, these cats are always underfoot. They love to be close to their owners and follow them from room to room. Gregarious and outgoing, they are quite active and love to run and jump. Most Tonkinese love visitors and will happily "chat" with anyone who will listen to them.

Tonkinese Blue Mink

Copper	Gold	Yellow	Light Green
Green	Aqua	Blue	Odd Eyes

To conform to coat color

Pointed Color							
Seal	Chocolate	Cinnamon	Blue	Lilac	Fawn	Red	Cream

Pattern								
Solid Color	Tortoise-shell	Agouti Tabby	Mackerel Tabby	Spotted Tabby	Classic Tabby	Silver	Tipped Color	Parti-Color

Turkish Angora

A true living legend, the ancient Turkish Angora may be compared with a ballerina, draped in long, silky fabric that moves with the wind.

General Description

The Turkish Angora is an elegant cat with flowing long hair. Long and svelte, the cat's foreign-type body is graceful and quick of movement. The Turkish Angora is thought to be the source of the long hair seen on many present-day cats.

History

The Turkish Angora, a natural breed, was the first longhair cat breed in Europe; it was brought from Ankara, Turkey, and introduced to France in the sixteenth century. Originally known as the Ankara Cat, this breed is thought to have originated from the Manul cat (Manul or Chinese desert cat *Felis manul*) that was domesticated by the Tartars. Some people believe it originally came from Russia.

In the early 1900s, in the beginnings of the "cat fancy" in Great Britain, the term "Angora" was used to describe any longhaired cat; the words "Angora" and "Persian" were used interchangeably. It is possible that the Persian actually got its long hair from the Angora as

Turkish Angoras were used for breeding with Persians. Soon, the Persian took precedence and the Turkish Angora almost disappeared from view. In the 1960s, Angoras were brought to the United States directly from Turkey, and the breed received championship status in the 1970s. Today, there are only a handful of breeders working with the Turkish Angora.

Appearance

The Turkish Angora is a semi-longhaired cat of medium size, foreign in type, with a firm body under its soft, silky coat. The head is a modified wedge, with two flat planes. These planes are formed by the flat top of the head and the line of the nose, meeting at an angle slightly above the eyes. The large, walnut-shaped eyes have a slight upward slant. The size and placement of the ears can make or break a Turkish Angora. They must be large, wide at the base, and set close together, high on the head and erect.

Turkish Angora Blue

Traditional Color									Sepia & Mink Color							
Black	Chocolate	Cinnamon	Blue	Lilac	Fawn	Red	Cream	White		Seal	Chocolate	Cinnamon	Blue	Lilac	Fawn	Red	Cream

Head: *modified wedge with flat planes.*
Body: *foreign.*

Copper Gold Yellow Hazel

Green Aqua Blue Odd Eyes

No relationship to coat color

Turkish Angora White

Turkish Angora Blue

Color and Pattern

The Turkish Angora comes in all colors, all divisions of the traditional category.

The whites are especially favored for their ethereal appearance and beauty.

One problem faced by breeders of Turkish Angoras (and other breeders of white cats) is the deafness that sometimes occurs in white cats. Some white Turkish Angoras with blue eyes, and some odd-eyed whites (cats with one blue eye and one amber eye), may be born deaf or partially deaf. Most odd-eyed cats can hear with the ear next to the amber eye, although this is not always the case. Please do not think that all white cats are deaf; this is not the case, as many are born with perfect hearing.

Temperament

The Turkish Angoras are elegant, active, intelligent cats. They are usually gentle, easygoing, and affectionate—often wanting to share their owner's bed and even the pillow. Everything about the Turkish Angora is "quick": this is a quick-witted, quick-moving, and sometimes quick-tempered cat. Turkish Angoras make playful, entertaining, loving pets.

Turkish Angora White

Pointed Color								Pattern								
Seal	Chocolate	Cinnamon	Blue	Lilac	Fawn	Red	Cream	Solid Color	Tortoise-shell	Agouti Tabby	Mackerel Tabby	Spotted Tabby	Classic Tabby	Silver	Tipped Color	Parti-Color

Turkish Van

Sometimes called "the swimming cat," the Turkish Van is known for its distinctive markings and its enjoyment of water.

General Description

The Turkish Van is a large, powerful, semi-longhaired cat with distinctive color markings around the ears and the tail, contrasting with its white coat. Unlike most cats, it loves to swim.

History

The Turkish Van is an ancient breed, found around the Lake Van region of southeastern Turkey. The Turkish Van cats must have quickly learned that if they swam out to meet the incoming fishing boats they just might be handed a free meal. This breed also developed a waterproof coat and two different hair lengths in order to adapt to extreme temperature changes.

Many of the early Turkish Vans imported into the United States were caged by their owners, which went against the independent, free-roaming nature of these cats. They resented their loss of freedom; they especially hated being placed in show rings at competitions. Consequently, the early Turkish Vans were known as unpleasant cats. Many of the breeders soon understood the cats' need for space and did away with the cages. The Turkish Vans of today are as pleasant as any other cat. Not many breeders are working with the Turkish Van, making these cats quite rare.

Appearance

The Turkish Van is a powerful, solidly built and muscular semi-longhaired cat with distinctive markings. The base coat is white, with a white blaze between the markings on the head, and white ears. The body is white; the color markings are restricted to around the ears and on the fully colored tail. The Turkish Van's cashmere-like coat is virtually nonmatting, making the coat easy to care for.

The broad head should be a modified wedge with rounded contours. The cheekbones are high and prominent; the large ears are turned slightly outward; and the large, walnut-shaped eyes are set slightly angled toward the lower part of the ear. The muzzle should be full and rounded.

Their bodies are long and broad; this is a full-chested cat with a substantial build. Indeed, Turkish Vans are considered one of the largest of the domestic breeds. As is the case with most of the larger breeds, they take three to five years to reach maturity.

Turkish Van Red Tabby & White

Traditional Color									Sepia & Mink Color							
Black	Chocolate	Cinnamon	Blue	Lilac	Fawn	Red	Cream	White		Seal	Chocolate	Cinnamon	Blue	Lilac	Fawn	Red	Cream

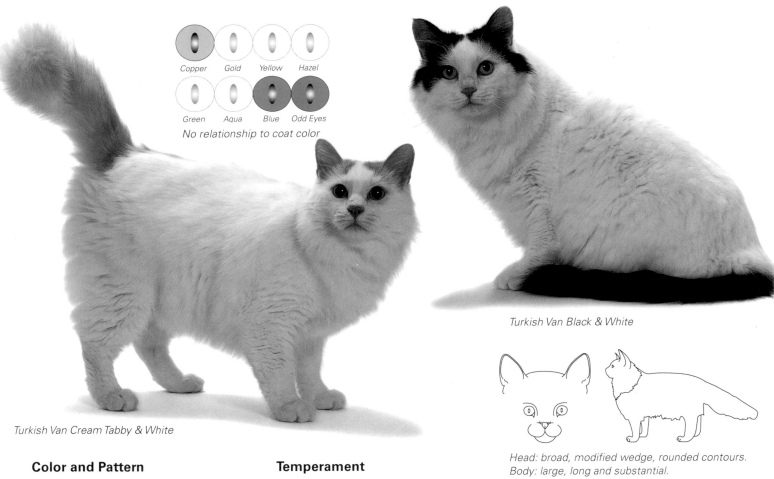

Copper | Gold | Yellow | Hazel
Green | Aqua | Blue | Odd Eyes

No relationship to coat color

Turkish Van Black & White

Turkish Van Cream Tabby & White

Head: broad, modified wedge, rounded contours.
Body: large, long and substantial.

Color and Pattern

The Turkish Van is shown in all colors of the traditional category, particolor division.

This cat is known for its distinctive coat pattern of auburn-colored head markings and tail on a chalk-white background. In its native Turkey, the white patch on the forehead is said to symbolize the thumbprint of Allah. Eye color is either blue, amber, or "odd-eyed" (meaning one eye of each color).

Temperament

This cat is strong, agile, quick, and striking in appearance, with an unusual affinity for being in water. Like the other "natural" breeds, the Turkish Van is a very intelligent cat with an assertive, independent attitude. This independence was necessary for the survival of this self-governing cat. Although they now live among people, these cats still need freedom to roam and come and go as they please. They make devoted companions once their loyalty has been won.

Turkish Van Tortoiseshell & White

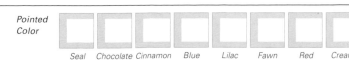

Pointed Color: Seal | Chocolate | Cinnamon | Blue | Lilac | Fawn | Red | Cream

Pattern: Solid Color | Tortoise-shell | Agouti Tabby | Mackerel Tabby | Spotted Tabby | Classic Tabby | Silver | Tipped Color | Parti-Color

American Bobtail

A short-tailed cat, which should be approximately 1 ½ to 6 inches in length and should not be kinked, the American Bobtail is seen in the shorthaired and semi-longhaired varieties.

The standard for this breed is currently being worked on and a new standard is in the making. Therefore, this description may not reflect what the breeders want this breed to look like. My description is based on the latest accepted standard for this breed.

This is a medium to large athletic cat that is powerfully built. The head is a broad, modified wedge, without flat planes. There is a gentle concave curve between the nose and brow. The brow should be prominent, with good length between the brow and the eyes. The cheekbones should be high. The muzzle should be somewhat square, but there should be no suggestion of it being foreshortened. A strong head, with an oval to almond-shaped eye set under a heavy brow, gives the cat a distinctive hunting look. The ears are medium to moderately large and are set as much on the top of the head as on the side. Lynx tipping is preferred. A thumb print on the tabbies is preferred.

In the shorthair, the double coat is of medium length. In the long-hair, the double coat is shaggy, semi-long hair.

This is a calm, intelligent, and easy-to-live-with cat.

American Bobtail Seal Lynx Point

American Bobtail Brown Spotted Tabby

American Bobtail Brown Spotted Tabby

Peterbald

The Peterbald is a 'hairless' cat with the body and head like that of the Oriental or Siamese. Like the Sphynx, it is not completely hairless in that it is actually covered with an extremely fine 'fuzz' like the skin of a peach or apricot.

Peterbald Blue

Peterbald Brown Mackerel Tabby

The Russians have a hairless cat they named the Don Sphynx. Some of the breeders felt that this breed was too large and heavy-boned. In order to refine the breed, they bred their Don Sphynx to an Oriental-type cat. This new type of hairless cat was not well received in the Moscow area but was loved in the St. Petersburg area, and was named the Peterbald. This breeding and exhibition of the Peterbald took place around 1993.

There are now catteries in the United States breeding the Peterbald. The Peterbald is an Oriental-type breed. The head is wedge shaped, the ears are large, the eyes are almond-shaped, and the body is of Oriental type.

This is an active, extremely friendly breed.

Peterbald Chocolate

Burmilla

The Burmilla was created by crossing the chinchilla Persian and the foreign Burmese. Not recognized in North America, it is considered either a separate breed, or simply a name for the shaded Asians, by various international cat registries.

The Burmilla has the medium-foreign body type of the Burmese and the color of the chinchilla silver Persian. It comes in either the shaded or chinchilla pattern, in four colors: black, blue, chocolate, and lilac. This is a short-haired cat with a short, dense coat that feels like raw silk at the tips. There are markings around the lips, the green eyes, and the brick-red nose, and a distinct "M" mark should appear on the forehead. There are delicate tabby markings on the head, legs, and tail.

This breed was first seen in England in 1981, as the result of an accidental breeding of a chinchilla Persian to a Burmese. The resulting kittens (four black-shaded female kittens) were so attractive that similar breedings were arranged in order to start a new breed.

The Burmilla is a friendly, outgoing cat. It is, however, not as noisy or demanding as the Burmese and tends to be laid back, like its chinchilla silver Persian ancestor.

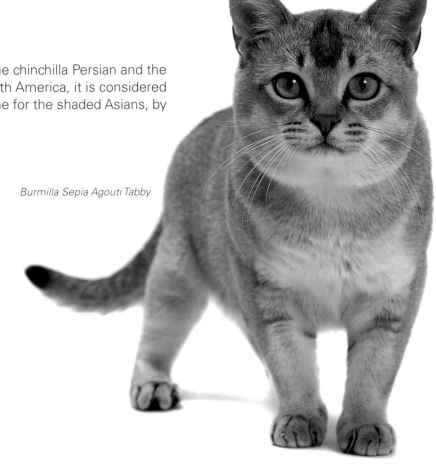

Burmilla Sepia Agouti Tabby

Burmilla Sepia Agouti Tabby

Household Pets

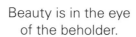
Beauty is in the eye
of the beholder.

The Household Pet Class is for cats that are not registered in the Championship Class. This class is open to any cat that is registered as a Household Pet; they must be altered in order to be shown in TICA.

We treat the Household Pets with the same respect and honor as the cats entered in the championship classes. They receive awards, titles, and International Awards.

The Household Pet exhibitors take great pride in showing off their beloved pets. A judging ring with Household Pets will always draw a large audience of other exhibitors and people visiting the cat show.

A moment to explain about the HHP Divisions. There are ten Household Pet Divisions: Solid, Tabby, Tortie, Pointed, Shaded, Solid and White, Tabby and White, Tortie and White, Pointed and White, and Shaded and White. The other rule of thumb is: If the cat looks like a tabby, it goes in the Tabby Division; if it looks like a solid, it goes in the Solid Division; if the hairs are "tipped," it goes in the Shaded Division; and if the cat has "points," it goes in the Pointed Division.

This is sort of a WYSIWYG class—What you see is what you get. It is a wonderful class of cats and kittens. Household Pet owners are very careful as to the cats they enter in a cat show. If the cat is unhappy about being shown, it is left at home. The cats are there because they want to be there. It is almost as if they have an inner sense that tells them "this will make my loved human companion happy."

The Australians have a name for the Household Pets: they call them *Companion Cats,* as that is what they are.

These cats may be of any color and pattern that nature creates. There is no one particular look. If Nature can produce it, you just may see it in the Household Pet Class. I always look forward to the challenge of judging this class. I never know what I will find; and I am seldom dis-appointed.

Household Pets are judged on beauty and condition.

Glossary of Terms

ABY TABBY OR AGOUTI TABBY
Agouti banding (ticking) paired with the least expression of the tabby pattern. The legs and face may show tabby markings ("M" on forehead, frown lines, bars). The tail tip should be the darker color. Stripes or bars should be considered a fault, although specific breeds may permit light pencil markings on the face, legs, or tail. Necklace tracings may also be permitted. (A/-, T^a/-)

AGOUTI
Ticked hairs, alternating bands of color on the hair; the agouti hairs are also found around tabby markings, making the tabby pattern visible. Controls the amount and distribution of melanin in the hairs. (A/-)

ALBINO
Devoid of pigment in the skin, coat, and eyes. (c/c)

ALLELE
One member of a pair of genes, or a series of genes, that can occur at a particular locus on homologous chromosomes. (C/-, c^b/c^b, c^s/c^s, c^a/c^a, c/c)

ALMOND-SHAPED
Refers to the eyes: having the pointed oval shape of an almond.

ALTERED
Describing a cat that has been neutered (male) or spayed (female).

APERTURE
An opening (such as an eye).

AUTOSOME
A chromosome not associated with the sex of the individual and therefore possessed in matching pairs by members of both sexes. Any chromosome other than the sex (X or Y) chromosomes.

AWN HAIRS
The coarser of the two types of secondary hairs, having thickened tips (bristle tips).

BALANCED
All the parts are in proportion according to the cat's breed standard.

BAND(S)
Refers to the phaeomelanin band in the hair. The phaeomelanin is "shredded"; a weakened phaeomelanin band. In the silvers, the Inhibitor gene removes the pigment entirely. Bands of ticked hairs.

BARRING
Tabby-striped markings.

BICOLOR PATTERN
A pattern consisting of a colored head, back, and tail with white on legs, feet, underside, and lower flanks. A white blaze such as the inverted "V" pattern is often seen. Various markings of white and pigment may occur, but the cat is generally one-third to two-thirds white. (S/-, P^b/-)

BLACK
Black color, with solid-color fur from the roots to the tip. (B/-, D/-, C/-)

BLAZE
A marking of color or white down the center of the forehead.

BLUE
Even gray-blue; lighter shades are preferred. Paw pads and nose leather are slate gray. Individual breed standards allow variations on blue, including Korat, Russian Blue, and Chartreux.
(B/-, d/d, C/-) (B/-, d/d, c^b/c^b) (B/-, d/d, c^s/c^s) (B/-, d/d, c^b/c^s)

BREADTH
The distance from side to side.

BREAK
A right-angle indentation of the nose below the bridge and between the eyes. The most extreme form of a change in direction. The Persian breed group is an example of cats that have a break.

BREECHES
(Britches) Long fur covering the upper part of the hind legs.

BREED
A group of domestic cats with similar type recognized by a cat registry and given a unique name for identification. A breed may be recognized by a registering body for championship status or registration purposes. Each organization has its own rules and standards for a breed.

BRIDGE
The upper bony ridge of the nose.

BRINDLE
(Brindles, brindling) The scattered "wrong"-colored hairs in the coat.

BROAD
Ample in measurement from side to side.

BRUSH
A bushy, generally long tail.

CALIBY
A pattern of torbie and white, or patched tabby and white. (A/-, P*/- S/-, T*/-, X/X^p) * = any pattern

CALICO
Tortoiseshell and white. (X/X^p + white spotting factor). Colors are blue tortie and white, chocolate tortie and white, cinnamon tortie and white, lilac tortie and white, fawn tortie and white. (a/a/-, P*/- S/-, X/X^p) *

CAMEO
A term used to describe the reds or creams and torties. Shell cameo is a shaded red; smoke cameo is a red smoke; smoke cameo tortie is a smoke tortie.

CARRIER
A heterozygous individual carrying a recessive gene. (A/a)

CAT FANCY
The group of people interested in the domestic feline in general or in breeding or show activities. There are registering bodies in almost every country; they register cats and litters, maintain a pedigree data bank, provide judges, and issue show licenses and club charters. In some countries these duties are performed by individual clubs.

CELL
A microscopic unit that performs the fundamental functions of life in the body.

CHAMPAGNE
A term used to describe a sepia or mink chocolate color.

CHINCHILLA

Coloring in which only the outermost tips of the hair are colored, the rest being silvery white or golden. The least amount of tipping. (A/-, I/-, T*/-, W^b/-)

CHINCHILLA or SHADED GOLDEN

Chinchilla golden is a gold to apricot undercolor, apricot preferred, with slight bronze or black tipping on the back, tail, and legs. The chin is a gold color. The belly may be a lighter shade than the back. Rims of eyes, lips, and nose are to be outlined with black, and the center of the nose is to be a brick red. Paw pads are slate gray to black. The tip of the tail should be bronze to black, as though dipped in ink. The overall effect is a lighter golden color than the shaded. Shaded golden will have more color on the tips of the hair. (A/-, i/i, T*/-, W^b/-)

CHOCOLATE

A rich shade of medium to dark chocolate brown. The color may be chestnut brown, medium to dark chocolate brown, milk chocolate brown, or coffee bean brown. (b/b, D/-)

CHROMOSOMES

The minute rod-like structures in the nucleus of a cell that controls inherited characteristics. The physical sites of nuclear genes, which are arranged in linear order. Each species has a characteristic number of chromosomes.

CINNAMON

A medium, warm brown with red overtones, similar to the color of a stick of cinnamon; lighter than the color of chocolate.(b^l/b^l, D/-)

CLASSIC TABBY

A tabby pattern mainly of blotches and swirls highlighted by a "bull's-eye" on each side of the body. The cat should show good contrast between the pale ground color and the deep, heavy markings. The head is barred with frown marks extending between ears and down the back of the neck to meet the "butterfly" on the shoulders, which divides the head lines from the spine lines. The spine lines are the wide, distinct stripes of dark marking color divided by stripes of paler ground color running from the butterfly to the tail. The swirl on the side of the body should be an unbroken circle of ground color around a spot of marking color. The legs should be evenly barred with bracelets coming to meet the body markings; the front of the neck should have at least one complete necklace, and the tail should be evenly marked with rings. The underside of the body should have rows of spots of the dark marking color, commonly called "vest buttons." (A/-, t^b/t^b)

CLOSE-LYING

Refers to the coat: lying very close to the skin.

COARSE

Lacking in delicacy or refinement. Not fine in texture; rough.

COAT COMPOSITION

There are three main types of hair that make up the normal coat: guard hairs, bristle or awn hairs, and down or wool hairs.

COBBY

Short and compact in body structure, with broad shoulders and rump. A cobby body usually has a short tail and a large, rounded head, as in the Persian, Himalayan, or Exotic Shorthair. The Manx and Cymric display the most extreme of the cobby body.

CONDITION

The state of health, both mental and physical, of the cat. Proper weight, overall health, and grooming are considerations.

CONFORMATION

The particular form of a cat; the size and shape of a breed. Also called type.

COW HOCKED

With the hind legs appearing to bend toward the center, knock-kneed like a cow, causing the feet to turn outward.

CREAM

A buff cream color, the paler the better; the dilute of red. (d/d, X/X^P) (d/d, X^P/Y)

CURLED EARS

The ears curl up and back, away from the face. The distinctive feature of the American Curl. (Ac/-)

DAM

Mother cat.

DEGREE OF CURL

The extent to which the ears curl backward, as in the American Curl.

DENSE COAT
Heavy, thick undercoat, with hairs crowded together.

DEPTH OF FLANK
The area between the rib cage and the thigh; determined by viewing the flank from top to bottom. The Manx/Cymric will have greater depth of flank; the Cornish Rex will have no depth of flank.

DILUTE
A paler version of a basic color, when the dense pigmentation is maltesed (pigment granules are clustered like a bunch of grapes): black -> blue, chocolate -> lilac, cinnamon -> fawn, red -> cream. (d/d)

DILUTE CALICO
Any of the tortoiseshell colors diluted (maltesed); the eumelanistic and phaeomelanistic colors maltesed. Colors are blue and cream; fawn and cream; lilac and cream; and blue, fawn, or lilac tortie plus the white spotting factor. (d/d)

DIPLOID
An individual or cell having two complete sets of chromosomes.

DOME
The forehead is well rounded, or domed out.

DOMESTIC
Often refers to the "street" cat; a non-pedigreed cat.

DOMINANCE
The expression of one member of a pair of allelic genes in whole (complete dominance) or in part (incomplete dominance) over the other member. (A/a)

DOMINANT
An adjective applied to that member of a pair of alleles which expresses itself in heterozygotes to the complete exclusion of the other member of the pair. The term may also be applied to the trait produced by a dominant gene. (A/a)

DOMINANT WHITE
White is the absence of color, the action of the dominant white gene. A masking gene. (W/-)

DONKEY EARS
Ears set too close together, creating the look of a donkey.

DOUBLE COAT
A thick top coat of longer hairs over a thick undercoat. The awn hairs are the same length as the guard hairs. The Russian Blue and British Shorthair, for example, have a double coat.

DOUBLE RECESSIVE
Having two pairs of recessive genes. (b/b, d/d)

DOWN HAIRS
Soft, crimped, secondary hairs.

EAR FURNISHINGS
Growth of hair extending horizontally from the ear.

EMBRYO
An animal in the early stages of development.

ENZYME
A complex protein produced by living cells that regulates or causes specific biochemical reactions in the body.

EPISTASIS
The condition where one gene suppresses the expression of another gene (and whatever phenotype it is responsible for), when the two genes are not alternate alleles of the same phenotype. The gene that does the suppressing is called the epistatic gene.

EUMELANIN
The black or brown-based melanin granules affecting pigmentation of hair, skin, and eyes; the granules may be dense or diluted (maltesed).
(B/-, D/-) (b/b, D/-) (b^l/b^l, D/-)
diluted = (B/-, d/d) (b/b, d/d) (bl/bl, d/d)

FAWN
"Coffee and milk" color, a warm pinkish buff. Cinnamon diluted (maltesed). (b^l/b^l,d/d)

FERAL
A domestic cat that has reverted to or has been born in the wild. These are not true wildcats, since they are of the same species as domestic cats.

FERTILIZATION
The union of the sperm and egg forming a single cell that will develop into an embryo; the embryo will develop into a fetus.

FINE
Very thin, slender, slim, dainty, svelte, lithe (when used to describe body type). May also refer to the type of hair.

FLANK
The part between the ribs and the thigh at either side of the body.

FOLDED EARS
The ears fold downward toward the face, due to a dominant gene affecting the cartilage. The distinctive feature of the Scottish Fold. (Fd/-)

FOREHEAD
The part of the face between the top of the eyes and the bottom of the ears.

FOREIGN TYPE
Body type characterized by a long body with legs in proportion to body length; slim, fine boning; long, tapering tail; modified wedge or wedge-shaped head with large ears and oval or almond-shaped eyes. The Abyssinian and Russian Blue have foreign type.

FROST
(In TICA, "frost" was renamed "lilac") Frost gray with pinkish tone; dove to light taupe gray; pinkish lavender. Chocolate maltesed. (b/b, d/d)

FULL
Rounded in shape; of generous proportions; wide. Having depth and body. The maximum or complete size or development.

GAMETE
A protoplast that, in the process of sexual reproduction, fuses with another protoplast.

GAUNTLETS
The white spotting pattern on the hind feet, usually ending below the hock.

GENE
The particulate determiner of a hereditary trait; a particular segment of a DNA molecule, located in the chromosome. Genes are units of heredity that control growth, development, and function of organisms.

GENE POOL
The total of all genes in a species' population.

GENOTYPE
The genetic makeup or constitution of an individual, with reference to the traits under consideration.

GERM CELL (GAMETE)
Ovum or female egg cell, or male sperm.

GLOVES
(Gloving Pattern) White on the feet, as seen in the Birman. (S/-, P^G/-)

GHOST MARKINGS
Faint tabby markings seen in some solid-colored cats, especially when young. Allowances are made for these markings when they appear on young kittens and sometimes even when found on young cats, according to individual breed standards.

GOLDEN
Color enhancer that changes yellow to apricot, as a result of the rufousing polygenes. A tabby may be a golden tabby or a chinchilla/shaded golden.

GROUND COLOR
The area of color on the lower part of the hair shaft; also the agouti area between the tabby pattern.

GUARD HAIRS
Long bristly hairs forming the outer coat.

HAIRLESSNESS
A lack of hair. It should be noted that hairlessness is not absolute in the Sphynx breed; hair may appear on the points; the body is covered with a light down. (hr/hr)

HARLEQUIN
One of the most extreme expressions of the white spotting factor. Color is limited to the extremities of the cat; several small patches of color are allowed on the body near the tail.
(S/-, PH/-)

HETEROZYGOUS
Having dissimilar genes received from each parent, of a given allelic pair or series, for a

particular characteristic. (A/a)

HOCK
The joint of the hind leg that corresponds to the human ankle. The joint between the knee and the top of the foot.

HOMOLOGOUS CHROMOSOMES
Chromosomes occurring in pairs, one from each parent, at the same locus on the chromosome.

HOMOZYGOUS
Having an identical pair of alleles for a particular characteristic. (A/A, a/a)

HONEY
A term used to describe the cinnamon color of sepias and minks.

HOOD
Mask of color extending to the base of the ear, forming a hood.

INBREEDING
Breeding within the immediate family of closely related cats: parent to offspring or brother to sister. This is sometimes intentionally done to continue a particular trait. Inbreeding must be done with great caution and knowledge of genetics.

INCOMPLETE DOMINANCE or PARTIAL DOMINANCE
The phenomenon in which the effects of both alleles at a particular locus are apparent in the phenotype of the heterozygote.

INHIBITOR GENE
The gene responsible for the inhibition of color and therefore the silver, as in the chinchilla and shaded silvers, and smokes. (I/-)

KITTEN CAP
A patch of color seen in Dominant White kittens and young adults, which may give a hint as to the color/pattern the cat is masking. This kitten cap will disappear when the kitten becomes an adult.

LACES
White on back feet.

LETHAL GENE
A gene whose phenotypic effect is sufficiently drastic to kill the bearer. Death from different lethal genes may occur at any time, from fertilization of the egg to advanced age. Lethal genes may be dominant, incompletely dominant, or recessive.

LILAC
Frost gray with pinkish tone; dove to light taupe gray; pinkish lavender. Chocolate diluted (maltesed). (b/b, d/d)

LINKAGE
The occurrence of different genes on the same chromosome that are inherited together.

LOCKET
A small area of white or color that is different from the desired body color. Usually refers to a white locket.

LOCUS
The position or place on a chromosome occupied by a particular gene or one of its alleles.

LONG AND SUBSTANTIAL
A description of the type of some breeds.

LYNX POINT
A pattern of tabby markings on the head, ears, tail, and legs of a pointed cat, such as in the seal lynx point or blue lynx point. The torso may be clear or may show a tabby pattern depending on specific breed standard. (A/-, c^s/c^s, T*) * = any tabby pattern

LYNX TIPS OR TIPPING
The extension of hairs from the tips of the ears. Lynx tips are desirable on the Maine Coon, for example.

MACKEREL TABBY
A cat with stripes running in a fishbone pattern, with no "bull's-eyes" or blotches. The sides of the mackerel tabby should be evenly barred with vertical unbroken lines of marking color similar to the rib bones of a fish, hence the name. There are three distinct spine lines, but they are very narrow and often meld into what looks like one wide stripe without fault. The head is barred with frown marks extending between the ears and down the back of the neck to meet the spine lines. Legs should be evenly barred with bracelets coming to meet the body markings; the front of the neck should have at least one complete necklace, and the tail should be evenly marked with rings. The underside of the body should have rows of spots of the dark marking color commonly referred to as "vest buttons." (A/-, T/-)

MALOCCLUSION
Faulty closing or meeting of the upper and lower teeth.

MALTESING
The clustering of pigment granules in the hair shaft. Also called dilution. See DILUTE. (d/d)

MARBLED
The tabby pattern presently associated with the Bengal. Similar to the classic pattern, but in place of a circle or "bull's-eye" is a rectangle that looks as if it has been stretched out or pulled at the corners.

MASCARA LINES
Dark lines of the indicative color that extend from the outer corners of the eyes.

MASK
Darker color covering the face, including whisker pads, that may be connected to the ears by tracings.

MELANIN
The main pigment that gives color to the skin, hair, and eyes. Melanin consists of eumelanin (X) and phaeomelanin (X^P).

MELANOBLASTS
Cells that will later form melanocytes.

MELANOCYTES
Pigment cells, located between or beneath the cells of the deepest layer of the epidermis, that synthesize melanin.

MELANOSOMES
Granules that produce melanin. Melanosomes are distributed throughout the epidermis and are responsible for the number, size, type, and distribution of pigment particles.

MINK
The result of the action of the pointed and sepia genes on eumelanin or phaeomelanin. Seal (natural) mink, blue mink, chocolate mink, cinnamon mink, lilac mink, fawn mink, red mink, and cream mink. "Mink" is used to describe the old Tonkinese colors as well as the mink colors in other breeds. (c^b/c^s)

MITTED PATTERN
A predominantly colored cat with white limited to paws, back legs, belly, chest, and chin in most specimens. White may also appear on the underside but should not extend to the sides of the cat nor around the neck area. (S/-, P^M/-)

MODIFIED WEDGE
In the shape of the head, defined by individual breed standards, the straight lines of the V-shaped wedge are changed. One example: curved lines and gentle contours, with the muzzle flowing gently into the skull; no flat planes; ears may be set slightly lower on the skull, as in the Abyssinian. Another example: a series of straight lines, including the forehead, the bridge to the end of the nose, the sides of the head to the muzzle, and the nose to the chin, as in

the Russian Blue. A final example: an equilateral triangle with straight lines, as in the Norwegian Forest Cat.

MODIFIERS
Polygenes that change the effect of a major gene.

MULTIPLE ALLELES
A series of three or more alternative alleles, any one of which may occur at a particular locus on a chromosome. The tabby system and the albino system are examples. ($C/-$, c^b/c^b, c^s/c^s) ($T^a/-$, $T/-$, t^b/t^b)

MUSCULATURE
The system of muscles of an animal or a body part.

MUTATION
A sudden change in genotype having no relation to the individual's ancestry. A change in the nucleotides on the chromosome.

MUTTON CHOPS
Fur that extends from the lower base of the ear past the jaw.

MUZZLE
The projecting part of the head, including jaws, chin, mouth, and nose.

MUZZLE BREAK
Indentation where the muzzle is attached to the skull; whisker break.

NATURAL MINK
Seal mink coloring.

NATURAL PROTECTIVE APPEARANCE
Describes the coat texture, water resistance, and hard protective coating of the hairs.

NECKLACE
Tabby markings in the neck area.

NBC
New breed or color. Also called AOV (any other variety).

NON-AGOUTI
The solid or self colors and tortie and smoke colors. The non-agouti gene prevents the formation of yellow bands; the hairs are of one solid color. Red is inopera-

tive on the non-agouti. Non-agouti can work only in conjunction with eumelanin; there is no phaeomelanin synthesis. (a/a)

NUCLEOTIDE BASES
A gene is composed of a series of nucleotide bases: adenine, guanine, thymine, and cytosine. The various alignments and repetitions form codes, which the messenger RNA is able to read and take to the cell for protein synthesis.

NUCLEUS
The command center of the cell, containing the chromosomes (DNA).

ODD-EYED
Having one blue eye and one copper, amber, orange, or green eye.

ORIENTAL SLANT
Eyes are slanted toward the nose; the outer corner of the eye slants toward the center or just below the center of the ear; projection of the line from the lower eye corner would extend to the center of the ear base.

ORIENTAL TYPE
A body type in which the head is long and triangular, the body is long and lean, the legs are long and fine, and the tail is long and whippy. The Siamese is of Oriental type.

OVERSHOT
Having an upper part projecting beyond the lower, as in an overshot jaw.

P*
Any of the white spotting patterns.

PARTICOLORS
Any color or pattern + white, seen in cats exhibiting the white spotting factor, regardless of the amount of white (except for lockets) on the basic background color. Any color and/or pattern in the other four divisions (solid, tabby, tortie, silver/smoke) may occur in the particolor division. Eye color should be the same as the corresponding coat color would be without piebald white spotting, except that blue eyes and odd eyes are also accepted. Blue and odd eyes are more likely to occur in cats with greater amounts of white. Paw pads and nose leather may be pink or the color associated with the body color. A paw pad or portion of the nose may be one single color or mottled with both colors. ($S/-$, $P^M/-$ or $P^B/-$ or $P^V/-$, etc.)

PATCHING
Clearly defined patches of color in the coat, as seen in torties and particolors (color/pattern + white).

PATTERN GENES
Refers to a specific pattern that is displayed when the White Spotting Factor is present and is of variable expression. For example, the Birmans have a Gloving Pattern. There are many degrees or expressions, from a small amount of white on a toe to the most extreme (Van Pattern), with all of the variations in between. ($P^M/-$ $P^B/-$, etc.)

PEDIGREE
The ancestral history of an individual; a chart showing such a history.

PHAEOMELANIN
The red- and yellow-based colors. Sex linked. (X^P/X^P = red or cream female) (X^P/Y = red or cream male)

PHENOTYPE
The appearance of an individual based on its genetic makeup.

PIEBALD WHITE SPOTTING
(White Spotting Factor) A factor that prevents migration of pigment cells, preventing formation of pigment in areas on the cat, thus forming areas of white surrounding pigmented areas. Premature melanocyte death. ($S/-$)

POINT COLOR
Darker color limited to the extremities of the cat's body: the mask, ears, tail, and feet.

POINTS
The extremities of a cat's body: the mask, ears, tail, and feet.

POLYDACTYLY
Extra toes. The normal number of toes are four on the front paws and five on the hind paws.

POLYGENES

Two or more different pairs of alleles, with a presumed cumulative effect, governing such quantitative traits as size, pigmentation, and intelligence. A small group of genes, when working together, can produce bodily characteristics. The determination of a given characteristic, such as weight or height, by the interaction of many genes.

PRICKED

Held straight up and alert in appearance (usually describes ears).

PRICKED SLIGHTLY FORWARD

Tilted or arched slightly forward, as if listening (usually describes ears).

PUG NOSE

Snub or upturned nose.

RANGY

Having a long body and slender legs.

RECESSIVE

The term applies to that member of a pair of genes that fails to express itself in the presence of its dominant allele. It also applies to the trait produced by a recessive gene. Recessive genes express themselves only in the homozygous state. (a/a)

RED

A deep, rich, clear orange-red; a terra-cotta or a burnt orange color. In TICA, red and cream cats are shown phenotypically and registered genotypically. (X^P/X^P female, X^P/Y male)

RESILIENT

Springing back to former shape or position; capable of recoiling from pressure.

REVERSED TICKING

A pattern of banding in which the outermost tip of banded hair is light instead of dark.

REX or REXED

Appearing to be without guard hairs (guard hairs are present but are shortened due to the rex gene; the ends may have broken off); the hair is wavy. Three rex genes appear in the cat fancy: the Cornish (r/r), Devon (re/re), and Selkirk (Sr/-).

ROMAN NOSE

The nose has a bump or arch; the nostrils may be set low. The Birman has a Roman nose.

ROMAN PROFILE

Downward curve, like the beak of a hawk, from the forehead to the tip of the nose. The Cornish Rex has a Roman profile.

ROSETTES

A variation of the tabby pattern whereby rosettes instead of spots are formed; results from a simple recessive gene.

RUDDY

The color in the Abyssinian or Somali is often referred to as ruddy. Bands are burnt sienna. Hair is ticked with two or three alternating bands of eumelanin and shredded phaeomelanin, the extreme outer tip to be the darkest, with the phaeomelanin band closest to the skin.

RUFF

Longer fur on the neck and chest.

RUFOUS

A polygene or the result of the action of a group of polygenes. The rufous factor, which may cause the "golden" effect, changes the drab beige-yellow band of the wild tabby to a brilliant apricot or burnt sienna color. The ruddy Abyssinian is a rufoused brown agouti tabby.

RUMP

The often fleshy hind part of the cat.

RUMPY

A virtually tailless Manx or Cymric (M/-). Ideally, a dimple should appear where the tail normally would be.

SABLE

Dark brown color, seal sepia. (B/-, c^b/c^b, D/-)

SCALLOPED

The white area on the feet (on the toes), as on the Ragdoll.

SEAL

The seal brown or dark brown color found at the points of pointed, sepia, or mink colors. (B/-, c^b or c^s or c^b/c^s, D/-)

SEMI-COBBY

A variation of the cobby body type; not short like the Manx, and not long like the Siamese. The British Shorthair and American Shorthair are examples.

SEMI-FOREIGN

A variation of the foreign body type, with long lines, medium boning, and modified wedge-shaped head. The Havana and Egyptian Mau are examples.

SEPIA

A color resulting from the action of recessive genes on eumelanin or phaeomelanin. The term refers to old Burmese colors, which are now found in other breeds. Variations are seal (sable) sepia, blue sepia, chocolate sepia, lilac sepia, red sepia, and cream sepia. (c^b/c^b)

SEPIA AGOUTI TABBY

Seal brown, dark brown, or sable brown ticking on a warm ivory ground color. The Singapura is a sable ticked tabby. (A/-, B/-, c^b/c^b, D/-, $T^a/$-)

SET AT A SLIGHT ANGLE

Refers to slant of eyes: slightly oblique, with the outer corner of the eye sitting a little higher than the inner corner.

SHADED

Coloring in which the tips of the hairs are colored, the rest being white or pale, the tipping being intermediate between chinchilla and smoke. Also referred to as the Shaded Division, which would include chinchilla, shaded, and smoke.

SHADING

Gradual variation in coat color, usually from the back to the belly.

SILKY

Silken, glossy, delicate, smooth, luxurious.

SILVER

Ground or undercolor has been silvered. The term applies to chinchilla or shaded silver, and silver tabby. Silver or silvering is the result of the Inhibitor gene that eliminates the yellow (shredded) granules in bands. A smoke or smoke tortie is also the result of the Inhibitor eliminating the shredded or weakened pigment granules at the lower portion of the hair. Examples are chinchilla or shaded silvers, silver tabbies, and silver torbies. (A/-, I/-, Wb/-)

SILVER LYNX POINT

Silver tabby markings are restricted to the points; markings are darker than non-silvered lynx point. All yellow is eliminated; the body is almost white. The cat may be tabby or torbie. (A/-, c^s/c^s, I/-, T*/-, wb/wb)

SIRE

Father.

SMOKE

The cat should appear to be of solid color until the hair is parted to reveal the pale or white undercolor. The hair shaft will have a large amount of color (three-quarters of the hair shaft) on a smaller amount of pale or white ground color. A smoke cat is a non-agouti (a/a) cat. (a/a, I/-, wb/wb)

SMOKE COLORS

The basic description is based on black smoke: the cat should appear jet black with a silvery white undercolor. Except for the silvery white frill and ear tufts on longhairs, the undercolor of the head, face, legs, back, sides, and tail do not show until the coat is parted. The belly and underside of the tail may appear gray, shading down to silvery white. (a/a, I/-, wb/wb)

SOLID POINT

The result of the action of the pointed gene on the solid and eumelanistic and phaeomelanistic colors. Color is restricted to the points. The body will be several shades lighter than the points. Seal point (a/a, B/-, c^s/c^s, D/-), blue point (a/a, B/-, c^s/c^s, d/d), chocolate point (a/a, b/b, c^s/c^s, D/-), cinnamon point (a/a, b^l/b^l, c^s/c^s, D/-), lilac point (a/a, b/b, c^s/c^s, d/d), fawn point (a/a, b^l/b^l, c^s/c^s, d/d), red point (B/-, c^s/c^s, D/-, X^P) , and cream point (B/-, c^s/c^s, d/d, X^P).

SORREL ABY

Cinnamon agouti tabby. A warm cinnamon brown ticked with alternating bands of burnt sienna and cinnamon. The tail is tipped with cinnamon. Paw pads are pink with cinnamon between the toes, extending slightly beyond the paws. In some organizations this color is called red but is not a true sex-linked red. (A/-, b^l/b^l, C/-, D/-, T^a/-)

SPOTTED TABBY

A tabby marked by spots of a darker color, most prominent on the sides of the body. The spots may vary in size and shape, but preference is given to round, evenly distributed spots. A dorsal stripe runs the length of the body to the tip of the tail. The stripe is ideally composed of spots. The marking of the face and forehead should be typical tabby markings; the underside of the body should have "vest buttons." Legs and tail are barred. The pattern may be caused by a separate gene, modifiers, or incomplete dominance of the tabby alleles.

STANDARD
The set of criteria established for a breed or color/pattern. Each recognized breed has a standard of perfection, which is usually made up by a breed committee and verified by the breed section. The standard is made for the ultimate in "perfection," but it is probable that no cat will ever completely measure up to this standard. The judge must compare each cat to the written standards for that particular breed and color or pattern. Breed standards vary between organizations and countries.

STOP
A change in direction; the short incline between the forepart of the skull and the muzzle, or a concave curve occurring in the nose at or just below eye level. The stop may be very slight or pronounced.

STURDY
Stocky, solidly built, thick set.

SYNTHESIS
The formation of a complex chemical compound by the combining of two or more simple compounds, elements, or radicals.

T*/-
Any tabby pattern.

TABBY
The tabby pattern is made up of two factors: the tabby pattern and the agouti (ticked) area between areas of the tabby pattern. Tabby patterns include ticked, mackerel, spotted, classic, and marbled tabby.

TAPER
A gradual decrease in thickness or width of an elongated object. To make or become gradually narrower toward one end.

TEXTURE
The appearance of the coat resulting from the arrangement and type of hair.

THERMOLABILE
Certain substances such as enzymes are destroyed or lose their special properties when heated to fifty-five degrees centigrade or higher (as opposed to thermostable). Tyrosinase, the enzyme responsible for melanin, is thermolabile. At full color, pigment develops to its fullest. The gene at the C locus mutated to the sepia and pointed genes, resulting in a pointed cat. Tyrosinase is heat sensitive. A seal point kitten, for example, is born almost colorless because it was kept warm inside the mother. The point color will develop on the extremities, which are the coldest part of the kitten.

THIRD JOINT
Equivalent to the location where the fingers are attached to the hand in humans.

TICKED or TICKING
Two or more alternating bands of color on each hair shaft, as on the Abyssinian.

TICKED TABBY
Ticking of the body hair with various shades of the marking color and ground color, the outer tipping being the darkest, the undercoat being of the ground color. The torso is of a delicate tweed effect. The tail, legs, and face may have tabby pencil markings. Necklace tracings are also seen in a well-marked specimen. In the Abyssinian and Somali, neck, leg, and tail markings are not desirable. Note: Ticked, Agouti, and Aby Tabby have the same genotype. (T^a/-)

TIPPING
Colored ends on the hairs, with a different color on the lower portion of the hair shaft. The degree of tipping can decide whether a cat is classified as a chinchilla, shaded, or smoke.

TORBIE
Usually a female cat: a tortoiseshell turned tabby, in which the black patches are tabbied forming a continuous pattern with the red patches. In a tortie cat, the eumelanistic patches will be solid; in a torbie cat, the eumelanistic patches will be tabbied. Also called patched tabby or tabby tortie. (A/-, X/X^P, T*/-)

TORBIE POINTS
Eumelanistic and phaeomelanistic patches of tabby markings restricted to the points. The body will be several shades lighter than the points. Usually shown with the lynx points.
(A/-, c^s/c^s, X/X^P, T*/-)

TORSO
The trunk of the body.

TORTIE
See TORTOISESHELL

TORTIE POINT
Body color: to be same as corresponding eumelanistic color point (i.e., seal tortie point—blue, chocolate, cinnamon, lilac, fawn). Shading, if any, is to be in same tone as points. It must be noted that body shading on the tortie point will be mottled. Point color will be a mottling of the corresponding eumelanistic and phaeomelanistic colors. A blaze is desirable. (c^s/c^s,X/X^P)

TORTOISESHELL
A mosaic of eumelanin and phaeomelanin patches, including the tortoiseshell, chocolate tortie, and cinnamon tortie colors. These colors may be diluted (maltesed) to produce the blue tortie, lilac tortie, or fawn tortie. The amounts of eumelanistic and phaeomelanistic pigment are randomly determined during embryological development. An evenly patched cat with good delineation between the colors and a distinct streak (blaze) of the phaeomelanistic color on the nose is preferred. (X/X^P)

TUBULAR
Cylindrical, shaped like a tube; having the same circumference at any point along its length.

TUCK UP
A curved spine creates the drawing in of the flank, as in a greyhound dog or the Cornish Rex cat; the opposite of depth of flank.

TUFT
A cluster of hair growing close together. Usually refers to toe tufts.

TYPE
Conformation; the general form and structure of the body. Different standards apply to different breeds.

TYROSINASE
An enzyme that acts with melanin to cause a series of biochemical changes.

UNDERCOAT
A true undercoat consists of the woolly or down hairs, under the longer guard hairs.

UNDERCOLOR
The part of the hair shaft closest to the skin. In a smoke, it is the unpigmented portion of the hair shaft; in tabbies, the ground color.

UNDERSHOT
Projecting out from below (as in a lower jaw that juts out beyond the upper jaw when the mouth is closed).

VAN PATTERN
Considered the most extreme expression of the white spotting factor. Color is restricted to the head and tail. One or two small patches of color on the body may be allowed. (P^V/-)

WALNUT-SHAPED
Having the rounded shape of a walnut; a slightly flattened circle, not quite an oval.

WEDGE
Refers to head shape as viewed from the top/front): the wedge shape is created by straight lines from outer ear bases along the sides of the muzzle, without a break in the jaw line at the whiskers. The skull is to be flat and the straight nose is a continuation of the forehead.

WHIPPY
Refers to the tail: long, slender, tapering.

WHITE
White is usually listed as a solid color; it is not a true color but the absence of color, the outcome of the action of the dominant white gene alone or together with the dominant white gene. Kittens and young adults may display a spot of color on the top of the head (kitten cap), showing the masked color or pattern. This spot usually disappears around eighteen months of age. (W/-)

WHITE SPOTTING FACTOR
A dominant gene of variable expression. The migration of melanoblasts from the neural crest is under the control of the White Spotting Factor. If there is no pigment in the hair shaft, the hair is white. The melanoblasts that are allowed to migrate will produce patches of colored hair. (S/-)

WIDE APART
Refers to distance between ears: more than one ear's width apart.

WIDE BAND
A dominant gene identified with the width of the band in ticked hairs. (Wb/-)

WITHERS
The highest part of the back; the area between the shoulder blades.

X
X = sex chromosome that does not have eumelanin or phaeomelanin genes as part of its chromosomal makeup. X/X = a eumelanistic female; X/X^P = a tortie female; X/Y = a eumelanistic male

X^P
Sex-linked chromosome that has the genes for phaeomelanin as part of its chromosomal makeup. X^P/X^P = a phaeomelanistic female; XP/Y = a phaeomelanistic male.

Y
Sex chromosome that determines if the individual is to be a male. There are no color genes as part of its chromosomal makeup.

photo by RAY PAULSEN

TETSU YAMAZAKI

•

Photographer Tetsu Yamazaki lives in Chiba, Japan, and his images have been published in books, magazines, and calendars throughout the world. Because of his understanding of and love for animals, cats and dogs seem to trust him, allowing him to create relaxed and natural portraits. His patience and persistence with even the most uncooperative cat always results in pictures that bring out both the beauty and the spirit of the animals—fans of his work often refer to the "Tetsu magic" in each of his photographs. His other work includes the best-selling *Legacy of the Dog*, also published by Chronicle Books.

GLORIA STEPHENS

•

Cats have always been a part of my life, ever since I was small, when my mother kept a cat as a pet. I have had many different breeds of cats in the past: Siamese, Oriental Shorthairs, American Shorthairs, Burmese, Abyssinians, Maine Coons, and Norwegian Forest Cats. I now keep Munchkins. When I went to my first cat show, I fell in love with a chocolate point Siamese I saw there, and I later came to own this beautiful cat. I became a breeder of Siamese and joined the cat club in New Orleans, where I lived at the time. I served as president of this club for many years, also serving as show secretary, entry clerk, and show manager at different times. After I moved to Oregon, I joined the Rogue River Cat Club, of which I am still a member.

I was accepted into the American Cat Fanciers Association's Judging Program in the 1970s. Beginning as a trainee, I advanced in the organization to become a full Allbreed Judge. I was subsequently appointed to the ACFA Jurisprudence Committee. When The International Cat Association (TICA) was formed in 1979, I left ACFA to become part of this new and innovative organization. I have been with TICA ever since, serving as allbreed judge, full instructor, judging administrator, genetics instructor, genetics committee member, judiciary committee member, and Webmaster.

My academic career has taken me into the fields of science and art. I have a Bachelor of Arts degree in Biology from the University of Mississippi; Bachelor's Degree in Fine Arts, specializing in Sculpture, from Sophia Newcomb, New Orleans, LA.; and a MAT Masters of Arts in Teaching, from Tulane University Graduate School, also in New Orleans, LA.

While studying at the University of Mississippi, I served as a lab assistant in many science classes, and also worked for the head of the Biology department as his research assistant on a Ford Foundation Grant to study regeneration.

I cannot imagine my life without cats. They are wonderful companions offering pleasures from having a cat to sit in your lap to the pleasure of running your fingers through its coat. And the reciprocal pleasure the cat receives from this, evidenced by its purr of thanks. Life is never dull around my household. There is something always new and exciting going on. If I have nothing to do, it is nice just to sit down among them and visit. It is a privilege to me to be owned by my cats.